MORPHING THE BLUES

THE WHITE STRIPES

AND THE STRANGE RELEVANCE OF DETROIT

MORPHING THE BLUES
The White Stripes And The Strange Relevance Of Detroit

by Martin Roach

A CHROME DREAMS PUBLICATION

WWW.CHROMEDREAMS.CO.UK

FIRST EDITION 2003

ISBN 1 84240 230 7

COPYRIGHT © 2003 Martin Roach

EDITOR   Rob Johnstone

DESIGN   Sylvia Grzeszczuk

Published by

CHROME DREAMS
PO BOX 230
NEW MALDEN
SURREY
KT3 6YY
UK

A catalogue record for this book is available from the British Library.

Printed in Poland

MORPHING THE BLUES

THE WHITE STRIPES

AND THE STRANGE RELEVANCE OF DETROIT

MARTIN ROACH

Acknowledgements

The author would like to warmly acknowledge the invaluable help and support of the following people who provided lengthy first-hand accounts of their part in the Detroit tale (in alphabetical order):

Andy at Flying Bomb, Ben Blackwell, Mick Collins, Jim Diamond, Gary Graff, Surge Joebot, Jeff Meier, John Peel, Matt Smith, Johnny Szymanski, Simon Wheeler, Neil Yee.

The author would also like to thank the following for their kind help (in alphabetical order): Mike Champion, Bernard Hernandez, Paul Hutton, Jez from KE, Louise Kattenhorn, Colleen Maloney, Peter Money, Nik Moore, Nigel at Rough Trade, Nita at Goldstar, Rob and Karen at Chrome Dreams

Very special thanks to Helen Hartley for her transcriptions.

Additional research by Richard Carman.

**"Dedicated to my son, Alfie Blue,
fell in love with a boy, October, 2002."**

PREFACE

There is so much mythology surrounding The White Stripes that it seems hard to filter out the fact from the fiction. They are brother and sister, they are man and wife, they only play and record on equipment pre-1963. They never have a set list. They only wear red, black and white, ever, even at home. They don't like music from any period later than the 1930s, and they create everything to revolve around the number three.

For the most part, many of these myths have been perpetuated by the media as much as the band themselves, but regardless of the original source, there is a great deal of misinformation about the duo that this book hopes to clarify.

The band were approached to interview for this work, but promptly and politely declined, preferring instead to "keep a certain sense of mystery about the band, which is why they're currently doing very, very few interviews." I was disappointed but not surprised and impressed with the respect and courtesy I was afforded by those around the band.

The problem may be that, by maintaining this sense of mystery, all they will achieve is to add fuel to the fire of misinformation. I am not suggesting they should co-operate with unofficial works like this; rather it is a moot point that in order to control the mythology around the band, they may have to volunteer more information than they feel comfortable with. Unless they do this, they risk being faced with a history that is re-written inaccurately and without their involvement. If, as Jack insists, a sense of history and honesty are the most important attributes of playing music, then that too might be the best course of action regarding his own life.

Once, when asked what it would feel like if every aspect of his and Meg's personal lives were common knowledge and their adoring public could watch them like some glorified rock 'n' roll soap opera, Jack earnestly but sincerely replied, "Then we are completely dead." If that is how he feels then, despite my own opinions on the band's relationship with their own history, he was right not to interview for this book.

While I have not had access to the band themselves, I have spoken at length a large number of the other key players in this fascinating saga. That in itself has been a delight and the people I have spoken with have been fantastically helpful. For that I am very thankful.

It is indeed a strange and fascinating tale. Through broken bones, doss houses, drag bars, camp-side fires, car crashes, human skulls, walls covered with animal heads and clocks, four hour car drives to travel eight miles and, oddly enough, upholstery, the story of The White Stripes is one of the most engaging and intricate of the modern era.

CHAPTER 1

"There is no doubt that 'rock 'n' roll music is the most dangerous thing that has ever happened. It is a monstrous threat. We must oppose it to the end."

Steve Race writing in *Melody Maker*, c. 1956.

The birthplace of The White Stripes is a tough town. Although the genesis of Detroit, such a gritty metropolis, might seem a million miles from the talk of Jack and Meg in the new Millenial multi-media world, the founding factors behind that city are the very building blocks of Detroit's social and community psyche. Without an understanding of where and how that city evolved, there can be no insight into any of the bands that have emerged from its loins.

Detroit has always been at the centre of American history and as influential in its own way as any other city on that vast and fruitful continent. It is a vibrant mix of innovation and introversion, whose repeated shifts from poverty to wealth and back again have given the city a reputation like no other. It is one of the true birthplaces of the modern world.

As far back as 1837, commentators and historians noted both Detroit's radical, explosive history and its contribution to American culture. "No place in the United States," reads the City Directory of that year, "presents such a series of events, interesting in themselves and permanently affecting as they occurred..." Formerly the capital of the state of Michigan, Detroit city lies on the north-eastern point of Lake Erie. Originally a village of native Americans, a fort was founded on the site of the modern city as early as 1701. Within a dozen years or so, the English, French and Native Americans had tried their very best to burn it to the ground.

A hundred years later, the city's first Governor, William Hull, found the city to be little more than a ruin. However, despite the ravages of war and fire, this vital strategic port - both militarily and economically - began to prosper, becoming a model city in the development of a young nation.

Detroit, and Michigan in general, have always been rich in resources, its farming industry being one of the most productive in America. Fruits, grain and dairy produce made the region wealthy as agricultural developments throughout the nineteenth and early twentieth centuries brought employment and prosperity to the city. Shipbuilding, pharmaceuticals and railroad manufacture added to the nascent wealth, while African Americans, Poles, Asians and Germans all spiced up the racial mix of the last years of the nineteenth century. But it was the fruits of a different industry that placed (and kept) Detroit at the centre of world affairs.

If Jack White had strolled down Woodward Avenue on March 6, 1896, he would have witnessed a momentous event. At a speed that would have allowed Jack to overtake him at a steady trot, Charles Bradley King and his mechanic Oliver E Barthel took to the road in the first gasoline-powered vehicle Detroit had ever seen. Similar vehicles had been developed in Europe, but King's horseless carriage was the first four-cylinder, single-block engine. A banal detail to a music-lover like Jack White perhaps, but one that would have epochal consequences for Detroit.

The infrastructure of other successful Detroit industries - shipbuilding, lumber, machine manufacture - meant that capital was already predisposed to investing in the new automobile industry, where skilled workmen were in high demand. At the turn of the century, Detroit numbered around 250,000 people. By 1930 it had risen to 1.6 million. Not only were the new generation of automobiles easier and cheaper to build, but new developments in building construction meant that the factories themselves were readily developed to keep pace with the rapid change in the fortunes of Detroit. River and railroad routes also allowed easy access to the city, which had soon nosed ahead of its neighbours in the development of the motor trade.

The few hundred men and women engaged in building cars at the turn of the century had increased to over 75,000 by 1920. Ransom E Olds took up the challenge of Charles King's earlier invention and founded Detroit's very first motor plant, followed shortly by Henry Ford, who - after a number of false starts - became Detroit's most famous son, and the name behind one of the first, great, world-wide brands - the founding of the Ford Motor Company in 1903 that brought him his fame and fortune.

Ford's installation of a production line is well-documented - what it meant to Detroit was that the city became synonymous with mass production, a concept that the <u>Motown</u> record label would emulate over half a century later, albeit in an altogether more artistic field. Yet even Motown's massive success paled in comparison to Ford's. By 1916, Ford was producing some 40% of all the motor vehicles on earth.

He was not a lone innovator. Some of the most famous names in the automobile industry were born in the Detroit area and its surrounding environs: as well as Ford and Olds, Hudson, Packard, Chrysler and General Motors can all be traced back in some form to the city.

Of course, such colossal industrial expansion had a seismic effect on the demographics of Detroit's population and, by definition, its social and cultural psyche. Throughout the early years of the twentieth century, migrant workers from overseas and from around the poorer states of America - especially the rural south - flocked to the city, as they did to other centres such as Chicago and Memphis. At the end of World War I, almost 20% of Detroit's population had been born outside of the United States. The city was evolving into a cultural melting pot within the space of two generations.

But periods of boom inevitably turn to stretches of gloom. The growth of production-line manufacture diluted the need for highly-skilled workers. As cheap labour flooded into Detroit, a constant battle between plant-owners and workers gave birth to the twin phenomena of industrial strife and trade union activism. Thus, the cataclysmic effect of The Great Depression of the early 1930s was felt in Detroit as harshly as anywhere else in the developed world.

During the war years, the city flourished again. As America was dragged into combat alongside Britain and France by the bombing of Pearl Harbour, so the car plants of Detroit moved seamlessly from automobile manufacture to supporting the war effort. More than half the tanks used by American troops in World War II came out of the Motor City, as Detroit had been christened; the city's plants produced three quarters of all the aircraft engines used in the campaign; nearly two thirds of the bombs dropped by US planes were built there and a staggering 92% of all the US vehicles used in the war were born and bred in Detroit City.

With so many indigenous Detroit men serving overseas, a social and economic vacuum was created which was easily filled by the previously suppressed minorities. Jobs were taken by groups of people previously

11

denied access to them, most notably from the female and black sections of society. Many managed to retain these jobs after the conflict had ended, thus emancipating large numbers of Detroit's previously under-privileged population. The first wave of Detroit's industrial development had empowered many to build and buy their own homes, now such 'luxuries' were afforded to those previously left at the bottom of the social heap.

Such a process was in keeping with another aspect of Detroit's past, whereby slaves from the south found liberty in Canada via the northern states and the so-called 'Doorway to Freedom'. The so-called 'Underground Railroad' movement was a network of individuals and institutions who, through stealthy support of fleeing slaves and the dodging of slave catchers, were at the forefront of the abolitionist movement. Detroit had been a vital point of escape for many African Americans. This historical migration added huge swathes of these oppressed itinerants' culture into the bubbling social cauldron of Detroit, not least the genetic blueprint for almost every genre of modern music, the blues.

Throughout the 1960s, Detroit was a touchstone for the social and economic developments of the American nation as a whole. The civil rights movement saw a notorious freedom march led by Dr Martin Luther King in 1963, down the Detroit street on which his namesake had driven that early automobile almost seven decades previously. Dr King even used the 'I have a dream' line famously employed in Washington two months later. Along with other cities across the country, Detroit experienced its own civil unrest with the street riots of summer 1967, sparked by a police raid on a speak-easy selling liquor beyond the legal licensing hours.

By the turn of the 1970s, dramatic changes – and a pervading sense of decline – were afoot in Detroit. In 1960 there were 700,000 job places in Detroit: by 2000 this had halved. In the twenty years to 1998, only 9,000 building permits were issued for new projects, while 108,000 buildings were demolished. As the heavy industrial plants upon which its wealth had been built declined and competition from overseas concerns became more effective, economic pressures saw many companies quitting Detroit, leaving an economic and cultural black hole in their wake. In 1990, the city spent $25 million destroying housing.

The architectural scars were but a mere flesh wound compared to the devastating effect this deteriorating economic health had on the city's labour force. At the turn of the new Millennium, the tenth largest city in America was comprised of 80% black households, almost a fifth of which earned less than $10,000 per annum; in the markedly more affluent suburbs, which were 80% white, the average household income was double that. According to the 2000 census, more than one third of the city's population was living beneath the accepted poverty level. Detroit is not a city used to luxury.

On July 23, 1701, Detroit had a population of zero. The following day it had a population of 100. By 1950, its population reached a peak of 1.8 million, and that has fallen steadily since, dropping to beneath one million in 2000 for the first time since 1920. The number of vacant property lots had also reached a staggering 40,000 by the turn of the millennium, ten times more than New York – a fact which would be used to ingenious effect by one of the key players in The White Stripes' story.

In many ways, Detroit is a shadow of its former self, yet it is still a city capable of huge cultural development that can have a worldwide influence. The White Stripes are the most relevant example of this innovation, but clearly not the only one. Back in the 1970s, Motown was followed by an explosion of garage bands, and from the lively FM radio scene of that decade emerged the Techno revolution of the 1980s.

And so that meandering, eventful and complex Detroit tale brings us to a cluster of bands nestling in the darkest, dirtiest and most deprived crevice of this unique city. Within that gaggle of eclectic musicians, there was a duo that was soaked in Detroit's history like the maggots in tequila bottles which so crassly represent the Mexican quarter where they lived. They hated much of that colloquial history, adored some of it and were unaware of the rest, but this did not stop them striking out and putting Detroit back on the global cultural map once again.

CHAPTER 2

"Modern music is three farts and a raspberry, orchestrated."

John Barbirolli

Along one entire wall hung a collection of clocks, each one competing with the next, yet all doing exactly the same thing, the cheapest as good as the most expensive. Scattered around this particular early twentieth century, three-storey wooden house were numerous items of odd furniture, each one individually made. Some chairs and benches had been bought from second-hand shops and refurbished, others simply found on the street and rescued from an ignominious grave in the county refuse tip. They were upholstered in a variety of fabrics and styles, but almost all in either white or red. This was the house that Jack built.

Until he was a young adult, Jack White's family had lived there too, in the working class Hispanic quarter of south-west Detroit known as Mexicantown, named like some homogenous themed restaurant. Jack White, nee Gillis, was the youngest of ten children brought up in a Catholic family. He did not have a sister called Meg.

Jack initially went to a Montessori infant school. "There was a drum circle," he later told *Rolling Stone*, "with all the kids passing around a little bongo drum. I was the last person in the circle and when it got to me I played 'Shave And A Haircut, Two Bits' - in front of all the parents. Blew the crowd away at five years old!"

Jack went on to attend a local high school that was predominantly black and whose relatively few white kids generally found themselves drawn into the rap and hip-hop culture that was increasingly prevalent. Except Jack. Jack did not like hip-hop. Or rap. It did nothing for him, so he didn't listen to it.

Rock was his vice, the price of which was being ostracised by almost all of his classmates. Led Zeppelin had ruled the world the year Jack was born in 1975 and for him they still held great interest. He was never bullied, but his musical preferences did not make his life any easier: "It would have been easy for me to give up and listen to (that music). At least then I would have had friends. But it just seemed odd to me for white kids to pretend to have a black accent, to pretend to be from the ghetto when they are from the suburbs."

In later years, when he was established as a rock star the world over, Jack still found no emotional sustenance in the soundtrack of his classroom years. "I find OutKast and Wu-Tang Clan interesting, but I consider music to be story-telling, melody and rhythm. A lot of hip-hop has broken music down. There are no instruments and no songwriting. So you're left with just story-telling and rhythm. And the story-telling can be so braggadocious, you're just left with rhythm. I don't find much emotion in that."

Like a million other rock kids, Jack wanted to be a drummer. Aged only eleven he acquired a basic kit and started to teach himself to play. It would be four years of beating the skins before Jack would pick up a guitar, which would also be entirely self-taught. By his early teens, he was recording very rough tapes of himself on both instruments through a four track reel-to-reel. He would ride around the grubby streets of Mexicantown on his dark red bicycle, humming the tunes he was starting to ferment in his head. When his bike was stolen, he was devastated ("one of the few times I cried over a possession"), but at least he still had his music.

His teenage mind was increasingly turning towards writing music and words. Both were invariably centered around his growing sense of being an outsider. He penned a poem called 'Image Can Kill Love.' "It was anti things that had no meaning behind them," he later told one reporter. "Things that were done simply because they looked or sounded cool."

Meg White (her real surname) looked cool. She wasn't into hip-hop or rap either. In fact, she wasn't particularly into music at all, flirting only briefly with a violin. A year Jack's senior, she had a sister, Heather, and lived in the same zip code as Jack Gillis – but not in the same family. By her own admission, she was something of a wallflower lacking both in ambition and confidence. It has been suggested that Jack and Meg first met at nursery school – which would make them childhood sweethearts – but this is hard to verify.

While Meg's school years are shrouded in mystery, there is more detail about Jack's educational career. He was an averagely good student, but was hardly a fan of school. "On the last day (of each school year), I would go outside and kiss the ground like the Pope does when he lands in a new country, but all the other kids didn't know about the Pope doing that so they would just make fun of me." It is unclear about Jack's family life around his mid-to-late teens - some articles quote him as saying his parents moved house and he decided to stay behind, with only a piano for company, which he then learnt to play too.

15

Some reports have Jack studying music at Cass Tech while others suggest he enrolled on a film course in 1992, with every intention of becoming a famous director. Whatever the course he participated in, he was desperately disappointed by what he saw as the immaturity of his fellow students and quickly lost interest. Meg also went to college - to study catering - but eventually ended up taking numerous bar-tending and waitressing jobs to pay the bills, including one at a blues bar in the trendy northern Detroit suburb of Royal Oak called Memphis Smoke (Cory, drummer with fellow Detroit band Electric Six also used to work there).

While he was still studying, Jack took up an apprenticeship working for an upholstery business owned by a certain Brian Muldoon, some sixteen years Jack's senior. At first, Jack was just the delivery boy and general gopher, but over time he started to learn the skills of upholstery itself.

He and Muldoon became good friends and the latter started introducing Jack to a much wider palate of music. Although six of Jack's brothers were reputed to have been in a local band called Catalyst, his musical knowledge at this point was very limited. Muldoon, a music fanatic, played Jack records by the Cramps, the Stooges, Velvet Underground and even Howlin' Wolf, to name but a few, and the pair started going to gigs and local shows. Brian and Jack also jammed often, with Jack playing drums to Muldoon's guitar. Although they just rehearsed, they christened themselves Two Part Resin, a term taken from Muldoon's profession. This was a precursor to a later garage-blues band they would form together, called suitably, The Upholsterers (only one record, a seven inch vinyl surfaced, the posthumously released 'Makers Of High Grade Suites' on the label Sympathy For The Record Industry).

Outside of these older reference points, Jack found little interest in more contemporary acts, although he has said that he loved Nirvana. Jack's job naturally led him towards an interest in furniture design, which in turn switched him on to art movements such as De Stijl and Bauhaus, both of which have featured in many bands material over the years.

In a characteristic that would go on to typify his dealings with the corporate machinations of the record industry, Jack found the commercial side of upholstering repulsive. By way of relief, he took to hiding poems inside the sealed-up backs of chairs he had repaired, a literary message-in-a-bottle for his future fellow craftsmen. "Poems to other upholsterers. They are the only people who see inside a sofa... and they won't get it for years."

A musical time capsule which Jack unearthed for himself was an obsession with the blues. Jack has mentioned many names who have influenced him over the years - Led Zeppelin obviously, but he also listened to AC/DC and Pink Floyd in his mid-teens. However, when he discovered Robert Johnson and other bluesmen, everything changed. That moment was his Year Zero. "That music made me discard everything else and just get down to the soul and honesty of the blues." One musician - perhaps more than any other - who had an indelible impact on his ideas and thoughts about music, was Son House.

Rock stars make a habit of referencing former musical acolytes - often quite deliberately in the hope of some caché rubbing off on them, other times genuinely - but few took that retrospective interest as far back as Jack White. In 2002, with The White Stripes' third album being avidly received by a fawning modern media, Jack was often found sitting in the corner of a smoky pub, microphone and journalist in front of him, talking about Son House, an artist who was born exactly one century before.

Son House arrived in the world in 1902 as plain Eddie James House Junior in Mississippi. He would live to the ripe old age of 86. Like so many seminal blues artists, House was from a deeply religious household and was drawn to the ministry in his early life, only taking up the guitar at the age of twenty-five. This conflict - between the feral nature and lifestyle of the blues versus his secular beliefs - fuelled a constant struggle and artistic tension in his work, something Jack White would suggest existed in his own music at a much later date.

However, thereafter ends all the obvious similarities between Jack and Son House. In 1928, House served a year in jail for manslaughter, having acted in self-defence. Twelve months after leaving prison, he was spotted by a talent scout from the Paramount label and recruited for some forthcoming recording work. What followed were legendary sessions alongside Charley Patton, Willie Brown and Louise Johnson. House's contributions are widely regarded as the work of a remarkable musician, one who thrived on raw passion and conviction so deeply that he shamed the lesser work of supposedly more technically-gifted peers. His ferocious barking vocals and astounding guitar work have since marked him out as one of the most instinctive players of all time.

His legacy did not stop there. He played shows almost nightly throughout most of the 1930s and even found time to teach blues masters such as Muddy Waters and Robert Johnson. In 1941 he recorded a solo record that was awesome in its diversity and ability, a landmark for anyone interested in the blues. By 1948, aged only forty six, he moved to New York and retired from music, a relative youngster in the genre. He went underground and almost twenty years later, was 'discovered', infirm, alcoholic and almost incapable of playing the instrument that he once mastered so beautifully. He worked hard to get back to his former greatness and managed to record an album for Columbia, which was avidly received by his legions of (predominantly white) fans. His physical and mental sharpness never fully recovered, however, and by 1974 he retired for the final time, moving to Detroit, where he died in 1988.

Jack's first encounter with Son House was the recording of 'Grinning In Your Face'. "There was truth in that record. I realised that less can be more too. Why get a bass player? Why add more stuff when it is already truthful?"

With Detroit's music history being what it is, the all-encompassing stench of the Stooges and MC5 was an influence that few bands could avoid (more of which will follow). To delve so deeply into the formative days of modern music immediately separated Jack White from his contemporaries. From a guitarist's point of view, what it also did was set a parameter that could never really be equalled - no matter how brilliant and gifted Jack became on the six-string, it was unlikely (and he would no doubt agree) that he could ever touch the genius of Son House. Jack's band The White Stripes would go on to cover House songs such as the menacing 'Death Letter', a testing tribute indeed, as well as 'John The Revelator'. Flying a little too close to the sun perhaps, but at least Jack had set his sights high. "We could do a great version of 'Death Letter', and if I was smiling and enjoying every moment of it, I don't think anyone would understand how much that song means to me."

"He's buried here in town," Jack later told journalist J. David Santen, "and I went to visit his grave at this little run-down cemetery. There's two empty spaces on either side of him - I'd like to get a hold of that burial plot (not that I deserve it), but that'd be a big honour to me."

Jack was around eighteen when he first heard Son House and other blues artists such as Robert Johnson and Muddy Waters. He was soon following the sprawling branches of the blues family tree to its most extreme corners - Robert Johnson listened to phonographs by Leroy Carr and Lonnie Johnson, so Jack checked those out too. Son House listened to Charley Patton's records so Jack bought some of those as well. House had also said he'd learnt much from a Clarksdale musician named

Lemon, who had in turn listened to Blind Lemon Jefferson 78s… and so on and so on.

Inevitably, this led Jack back to natural ancestral links some of which he was already familiar with – for example Led Zeppelin - others who were yet to be discovered, such as Bob Dylan and Cream. Before long, his previously rather narrow record collection had started to develop some very intriguing niches. As with many young musicians, Jack's selection was severely limited by finances. Fortunately, when some friends of his took up jobs at a local record store, he was able to get discounts and therefore feed his growing hunger for new sounds.

Records by Cole Porter and Johnny Cash represented yet another sonic diversion, but it was the blues that enthralled him most of all. "I think that song structures of the 1920s and 1930s were so accessible to people," Jack has said. "Melody was so important. Not that it isn't in pop music today, but it was on a more basic, simple level back then. That kind of music has the appeal of a nursery rhyme."

CHAPTER 3

"A combination of rats, roaches, love and guts."

Motown founder Berry Gordy defining his record label's sound.

Oddly enough, Jack's ever-widening tastes had very little to do with the key figures in Detroit's musical history, specifically the Motown record empire, the Stooges and the MC5. However, any study of the music scene in that city would be redundant without some analysis of those three wise men of Motor City music. Furthermore, although The White Stripes may not consciously attribute their style or influence to any of these three factors (although Jack does acknowledge passing interest in the latter two), it is hard to believe that any band from Detroit can exist without some hint – even subconsciously - of any or all of them (just as no band could ever come out of Liverpool without mentioning or being aware of the Beatles).

Jack has said many times that he actively disliked Motown. Nonetheless, that genre/record label had a huge impact on both Detroit and the music industry around the world. Its history is relevant to the White Stripes tale for two reasons. Firstly, it establishes the cauldron in which that duo developed. Secondly, there is a musical link, in that Motown's songs were so economical, so pared down to only what was absolutely necessary. That label rarely committed a sound to tape unless it made a contribution to the overall sound. Same goes for The White Stripes. You could also stretch the comparison a little more by highlighting the lack of ego in the music and its priority over the actual personnel, again something which Jack strives for.

Once again, we must delve back into the history archives, this time to the aftermath of World War I. Berry Gordy II made a deal in Detroit selling timber stumps and moved to the city alone but brought his family to join him soon after - a process known as chain-migration. Unlike many contemporaries, Gordy had no intention of joining the swarms of workers buzzing around the honeypots of the motor industry. Berry Gordy was set on building his own business up from nowhere.

Berry's seventh child, Berry Jnr. (born Nov 28 1929), was six years old when his father and mother established a successful painting and decorating business and a grocery store, named after the black educator Booker T Washington. The future head of Motown learned much about business from his parents, learned to play the piano from an uncle, and grew up watching the bustling street life of pimps, blues singers and hookers from the colourful Eastside.

A bright kid, Berry Gordy Jnr was a born hustler - he sold newspapers, shined shoes and hawked a singer door-to-door all as means of making money alongside what his father paid him for working in the family business. Music and boxing soon became his passions. Although he appeared on the same bill as the legendary black fighter Joe Louis, in 1950 he decided that - as a boxer might only work once every three or four weeks, while musicians could earn a buck every night of the week - it would be the musical road he would follow.

Berry Gordy Jnr's first recording was a commercial for his brother's printing firm, a one-minute radio song in the style of Nat King Cole. Soon after, he was drafted and served in the Korean war, on his return home he followed the trends of his entrepreneurial family and opened The House of Jazz, a record store in Eastside, which went bust in 1955. A series of dead-end jobs followed - including the almost obligatory stint in the car plant.

One of the most important venues for black music in Detroit at the time was the Flame Show Bar. Billie Holiday, T-Bone Walker and other great black singers appeared here and Berry's sisters, Gwen and Anna, had the concession for photographing stars there. The club's owner, a manager of acts such as Jackie Wilson, invited Gordy to write songs for the artists that he controlled. Gordy found himself co-writing at the Pearl Music Company on Alexandrine Street. While voices such as Aretha Franklin - then an unknown gospel singer - Freda Payne and LaVern Baker were on the up, Berry, along with his co-writers Roquel Billy Davis and sister Gwen, struck gold with a song written for the great Etta James. 'All I Could Do Was Cry', released on Chicago's legendary Chess label, which topped the R&B charts.

By this time already married, divorced and in his mid-twenties, Berry shared the writing of 'Reet Petite' for Jackie Wilson - a performance that Gordy described in his 1994 autobiography *To Be Loved* as a 'so-so song' that Wilson turned into a classic. The team followed up with the ballad 'To Be Loved' itself, another hit for Wilson. A chance meeting with a young William Robinson then led to one of the greatest partnerships in music history. Two driven young men with a passion for music and a determination to hone their craft to perfection, Berry Gordy and 'Smokey' Robinson started a ball rolling that led to the formation of Motown when their first recording together was released on End Records in February

1958. 'Got A Job', their first single, and 'My Mama Done Told Me' were recorded in one day at United Sound Studios – surprisingly swift even for that era. The band's name of the Miracles was pulled out of a hat to replace their earlier name of the Matadors, and a recording legend was born.

A group of aspiring singers and writers completed this formidable team, many of whom who would become part of the Motown magic. On a family loan of eight hundred dollars Gordy also founded Tamla (named after the Debbie Reynolds hit 'Tammy') to release 'Come To Me' by Marv Johnson. 'Come To Me' – licensed to United Artists - was Tamla's first release, and made Gordy a hit producer as well as a hit song writer. Motown - a contraction derived from Detroit's nickname of Motor City - was the second label. It was originally intended that Tamla would carry solo artists and Motown would carry the groups. 'Tamla Motown' was formed later to handle the company's overseas sales.

The Tamla-Motown group of record labels became a legend in popular music history, one of the most important labels of all time and a model for independents for decades to come. Its roster of stars, based at the company offices of Hitsville - Gordy's aspirational name to describe just exactly what his business was all about - became the most successful in the American record industry within a handful of years. Gordy finally found a format that allowed his vision to blossom, as he could afford to install his own studio facilities, sales department, publishing and all departments together - a Detroit 'production line' of sound. One of the first songs recorded there was 'Money (That's What I Want)', a wonderful beast of a song that became a standard for the Beatles and a post-punk hit for the Flying Lizards.

New faces arrived almost daily to get a taste of the new label. Mary Wells, Marvin Gaye, Stevie Wonder, the Supremes, the Temptations, the Four Tops, the Marvelettes, Martha and the Vandellas, The Miracles... the list seems endless. And such great songs: 'You Really Got A Hold on Me'; 'Tears of a Clown'; 'Dancing In The Streets'; 'My Guy'; and - a deliberate follow-up, but such a beautiful and different song from Mary Wells' original - 'My Girl'. Nobody with a love of music, whether classical, punk, heavy metal, folk or opera, could fail to be moved by the incredible energy, the fabulous vocal performances, the tight-as-a-fist arrangements and the sheer unbridled enthusiasm of these early releases from Motown. Gordy's aim - to hook people for good within twenty seconds, or not release the record - rarely failed.

Detroit rapidly became the home of a nationwide phenomenon as the Motown Revue began touring the States and abroad. By Christmas 1968, Motown could claim five of the *Billboard Top 100* top ten singles, holding down the highest places for over a month - an unprecedented achievement. With the Supremes, and particularly with Diana Ross, Gordy struck even more pure gold. Yet better still was to come. Diana Ross then helped launch Motown's greatest discovery – the Jackson Five.

Unfortunately, throughout the 1970s, Motown's fortunes waxed and waned. Gordy focused heavily on the solo career of Diana Ross, while many of the top acts defected to other labels, culminating in the Jackson 5 moving to Epic in 1975. Ross herself moved to RCA in 1981, and despite top sellers from acts such as Lionel Richie, the Commodores, Stevie Wonder and Marvin Gaye, as Motown entered the 1980s there were a rash of law suits and business difficulties. The gradual drift of Motown's operation to the west coast in the 1970s and 1980s mirrored further changing fortunes from the Motor City. Finally, in 1988, MCA and Boston Ventures bought the company for $61 million.

If the history of Detroit is written according to its worldwide achievements, then Motown - along with the motor industry - can rightly claim to be its greatest export. Like the motor trade, Motown was a factory, a system whereby an unknown kid could bring his talent in off of the street and walk out a star. Motown allowed young black musicians to fight it out in the hitherto white world of national pop stardom. Motown influenced pop music internationally, affecting the British beat boom as much as did Elvis, Little Richard and Chuck Berry. All those ingredients made for a second wave of music in Detroit, itself influenced largely by the Beatles and the Rolling Stones - from which emerged another wave of internationally-known acts including the MC5 and - most importantly - the mighty Stooges.

Jack didn't like Motown: "I know that's blasphemous when you are from Detroit, but I was never a fan. I don't care for the production much." He was, however, like many people in Motor City, a fan of the Stooges and the MC5. Jack once said: "The Stooges *Fun House*, even though they were from Ann Arbor, that just feels like Detroit to me. I'm not trying to sound romantic about the city or anything, but it's like you can do anything you want here, you can come up with an artistic idea and you can actually get it across to people, where as I'd say New York or LA you can't do that because there's too much going on, there's too many different kinds of areas in the city and there's like 50,000 bands or artists or painters, it must be so hard to get an idea across."

Though for many Motown represented the zenith of Detroit's musical contribution to the world, the next generation of musicians in the mid-1960s took their inspiration from the British invasion of bands from the Beatles onwards, including, of course, the Rolling Stones, the Kinks and the Animals. The Beatles played Detroit twice, to incredible scenes never seen before in the city. On their first tour of America in 1964 they packed out the Olympia Stadium on September 6. The same venue saw them winding up their live career, as, shortly before their final, wire-caged performance in California, they returned to Detroit in August 1966. The tight harmonies, gorgeous melodies and sparkling arrangements of Motown were inspiration enough, but with the Beatles came a guitar-led sound, heavy monotone beat and frantic energy, played by its own creators, with no apparent team of writers, arrangers and money-men in support.

The message was clear - 'go forth and form your own band.' Basic guitar, bass and drums became the template of many of the bands who followed, and with the decadent influence of the Stones added to the brew, many of the garage, hippy and proto-punk outfits took a turn down a far darker and more sinister road than it appeared the Supremes would ever follow…. music in the Motor City was changing fast.

With Motown still in full swing, this aforementioned arrival of the Beatles had fuelled a new wave of bands in and around the Detroit area. In the early 1960s, apart from Motown, there wasn't much of a record industry in Detroit, and venues for bands were hard to find. Consequently there were few groups active in the city, and it was radio DJs who became the local celebrities.

Ironically, as the release of *The Beatles' Second Album* would show, this bright, witty and unfeasibly talented Liverpudlian outfit was itself much influenced already by the sounds of black Detroit: three Motown songs graced that album and its transatlantic counterpart, the UK release *With The Beatles*. 'You Really Got A Hold On Me', 'Money (That's What I Want)' and 'Please Mr Postman' illustrated how much The Beatles' own tight harmonies, stomping arrangements and in-your-face showmanship already owed to Detroit. But in return, the Motor City took something else from the Fab Four.

With the Beatles had come a rough, laddish, guitar-based sound: heavy, on-the-beat drumming, and little in the way of fancy arrangements beyond what a four-piece band could offer. While Motown continued to provide a home for many black artists, most Detroit white kids took

24

the inspiration of the Beatles to create their own grungy, punky sound. Promoters realised that there was a demand for live bands who could give the punters a little slice of Beatlemania locally, or who could riff out a Rolling Stones-style set instead (the Stones had played at the Olympia Stadium themselves in June 1964). It wasn't just these two groups either - behind them came an invading force so powerful that, where pop music in America had previously been dominated by American acts, now it was records by the Beatles and the Stones, the Kinks, Them, the Who and the Animals that found favour. Clubs such as The Hideout, The Club (in out-of-town Monroe), The Eastown and The Pumpkin gathered a mixed crowd of straight-from-work teenagers in leathers and denim, hungry for the newest rock 'n' roll.

Kids like Ted Nugent - in the 1970s a multi-platinum-selling act - formed bands one day and split them the next. Born in 1948, Nugent formed his first group in 1960 and is best known perhaps for his intricate guitar work – yet back when he was in a band called the Royal High Boys, he was accompanied only by a drummer. The White Stripes they certainly weren't, and they did indeed soon add a bass player, vocalist and second guitar, renaming themselves the Lourdes. However, it does show that Jack and Meg are certainly not the first Detroiters to experiment with such a line-up.

Other bands in and around Detroit in the early- and mid-1960s included the High Tones, who, via their singer Ron Stults and a number of line up changes (Stults also fronted the Village Beaus for a while) became the Unrelated Segments, who lasted throughout much of the mid-1960s. Tim Tam and the Turn Ons, the Shy Guys (who opened for the Dave Clarke Five in 1966), the Human Beinz, the Wanted (who covered Wilson Pickett's 'In The Midnight Hour'), the Tidal Waves and the Southbound Freeway (one of the earliest pyschedelic bands in the wake of Hendrix's seminal *Are You Experienced*) were all a part of a very happening scene of British-invasion-influenced bands. Many began by emulating the Stones and the Beatles, moved on through Byrds motifs, and became the core of the hippy/acid scene. Of the same vintage, the Pleasure Seekers were an all-girl band featuring the teenage Suzi Quatro on bass, whose touring schedule went so far as a trip to Vietnam to entertain the troops.

Billy La Vere (born William Levise) fronted Billy Lee and the Rivieras, whose one 45 release gave little indication that, as Mitch Ryder and the Detroit Wheels, they would became one of the finest US bands

25

of the era, creating a blend of Motown and rock 'n' roll that works to this day. Ryder's next band, Detroit, teamed him up with Bob Ezrin and Steve Hunter, producer and guitarist associated with Lou Reed (*Berlin*) and Alice Cooper (another local boy, born Vincent Damon Furnier in Detroit, 1948). Also associated with Reed and Cooper (seminally on the latter's *Welcome To My Nightmare*) was Dick Wagner, guitarist with late 1960s Detroit band Frost, regulars around the Detroit and Michigan scenes from 1964 onwards.

A veritable melange of talent then. High energy rock 'n' roll bands, it seemed, responded well to the 1960s Detroit air – just as they would in the late 1990s. Spewed forth from this lineage that took them back through the Beatles and indirectly back to Detroit via Motown, and indeed most pertinent to The White Stripes' story, are the MC5 and the Stooges.

Fred 'Sonic' Smith and Wayne Kramer met at Lincoln Park High School, and shared a passion for guitar playing. Joined by 'friend of friend' Rob Tyner, after a number of line-ups, during which period Tyner left and re-joined the band, the three found themselves playing together in the Bounty Hunters. By 1965 they had become the Motor City Five, with Pat Burrows and Bob Gaspar on bass and drums. With a standard set comprising Stones, Motown, Chuck Berry and other covers, the band hooked up with local DJ Jerry Goodwin, who fixed them with a twenty-minute slot between records at his Saturday night gigs around Detroit. Hooked on traditional rock 'n' roll, the band was also heavily into improvised jazz, and - coining the phrase 'avant rock' - they developed a raucous, free-form, feedback-loaded stage set that could clear a ballroom before you could yell 'Long Tall Sally'.

As a covers band, the MC5 (as they had now become) supported the Dave Clarke Five, Motown group the Elgins, Stevie Wonder and Marvin Gaye, with new members Michael Davis on bass and Dennis Thompson on drums. Becoming local favourites, their first single, a cover of Them's 'I Can Only Give You Everything', of which only 500 copies were pressed, again shows the depth of the British influence on US pop. The band met and became associated with radical local journalist, DJ, artist, writer and activist John Sinclair, a former academic who had a huge influence on the MC5, introducing a political element to their music that lifted them out of the regular run of garage bands and put them on a platform at a time when the civil rights movement and anti-Vietnam activism made America a socio-political melting pot.

26

Signed to Elektra alongside one of their favourite local bands the Stooges, the MC5's new record deal led to one of the most infamous and oft-quoted live records ever made. *Kick Out The Jams*, their first album, was recorded at Detroit's Grande Ballroom, and released in February 1969. Two-chord wonders, nods to the Who, the Kingsmen, the Troggs and any number of other garage bands - the album confused as many as it enamoured. Lester Bangs famously trashed it in *Rolling Stone*; Hudson's department store in Detroit refused to stock it because of the foul language therein, and when the band placed an ad in the paper inciting fans to kick down the door of the store if they couldn't buy the album ('Fuck Hudson's' ran the ad!), they found themselves dropped by their record label with immediate effect. Although the initial pressings of the album contained the famously quoted line 'kick out the jams, motherfuckers', the line was rapidly amended in response to complaints to '...*brothers and sisters*'.

With a rebellious lifestyle to match, the careering MC5 were picked up by Atlantic Records, who released *Back In The USA* in late 1969. Peaking at 137 on the Billboard charts, the album reflected the chaos of the band. Lacking true direction, it included some fabulous, swaggering rock and roll, and also displayed a discipline beyond the live nihilism of the first album.

After successful tours abroad – including rabidly received sets in the UK – and no longer linked with Sinclair, by 1971's *High Time*, time was running out on the MC5. This, their third album and only their second studio release, was another confused and confusing affair. While each member contributed material, the record seemed yet again unsure of its right to rock or to experiment, and while reviewers in general were favourable, and its first side contained some classic stuff, the band were clearly fizzling out. The following year their brief, blistering flame was extinguished as Tyner and David left the band. A vestige of the MC5, still including Kramer and Smith, played their last gig on New Year's Eve 1972, back at the Grande Ballroom, Detroit.

As so often happens, their influence seems greater in hindsight than perhaps it was at the time. Genuinely feted by many as America's most exciting band of the moment, the MC5 sold relatively few albums. At a time when lead singers became more and more 'the front' of the band (The Stooges felt that Iggy left them behind, while 'Alice Cooper' transformed from a band of that name to a guy called Alice with a band behind him), the MC5 represented a real band of people working together for a cause. They wore their politics on their sleeves right next to their improvisational hearts, and stood for something artistically, musically, politically outside the contemporary mainstream. Constantly in trouble with the law - victims of the Republican paranoia of the 1960s and 1970s - their punk attitude from day one was clearly reflected in the UK movement that developed within four years of their demise, most notably with The Clash. By the time The Clash were instigating their own White Riots, there was a format established for bands like them - a trail blazed to some degree by the MC5. For the Five themselves, there was no established path to follow, and laying it down was perhaps their greatest legacy.

The fortunes of the MC5 were mixed following their split. Fred Smith went on to marry Patti Smith, after forming Sonic's Rendezvous with ex-Stooge Scott Asheton. He died of heart failure in 1994. Rob Tyner's heart gave way too, in 1991 – Jack White has often said his squealing vocals have been a big influence. Davis re-appeared in the mid-1970s in the 'anti-rock' band Destroy All Monsters, with Ron Asheton of the Stooges, who also joined up with Dennis Thompson in the Detroit band New Order (not the post-Joy Division British group) and, later, New Race. Wayne Kramer, looking svelte, middle-aged and happy with his lot, still gigs and releases critically acclaimed albums today.

If, with hindsight, the MC5 represent a great idea for a band that burned out before it quite fulfilled its potential, then their Ann Arbor (a town close to Detroit – more of which below) stablemates The Stooges certainly had a more lasting influence and - in Iggy Pop - gave the world a true rock 'n' roll icon. Every band coming out of Detroit owes The Stooges a debt of thanks for reminding the world that their city is made of more than cars and Motown. From The Stooges onwards, Detroit meant raw, destructive rock glamour of the first order. Detroit meant guitars. Stage presence. Cool. Blood. Sweat. And tears. Fellow Detroiter Alice Cooper took this lesson to pantomime lengths through the 1970s and 1980s, but Iggy and the Stooges invented, lived and survived the myth.

Famously born James Newell Osterberg in April 1947, the future Mr Pop was born of a good vintage, the son of a high school teacher and a housewife. Six months either side of Iggy's birth were born David Bowie, Marianne Faithful, Patti Smith, Warren Zevon, Steve Marriott, Elton John, Emmylou Harris, Brian May, Carlos Santana, Don Henley and many other post-war scene-changers. Raised in Ann Arbour, MI, Osterburg was an intelligent, studious kid, but by 1965 he was drumming in his high school band, the Iguanas. Although he graduated and took one semester of anthropology at University of Michigan, music was already in his blood. Taking from the Iguanas little more than his new nickname 'Iggy', Osterberg joined the Prime Movers, a white blues band more Rolling Stone than Beatles, more Howlin' Wolf than Herman's Hermits. He sat in on a number of bands around the Detroit music scene, including Motown groups such as the Four Tops, while by day he worked at the Discount Records store.

In 1966 Iggy moved to Chicago in search of more authentic blues, but by spring of '67 he was back in Detroit. Sharing with them a love of the Rolling Stones, Iggy joined up with former Prime Mover Ron Asheton (guitar) and his brother Scott (drummer of Detroit band the Chosen Few), and formed the Psychedelic Stooges, playing their first gig on Halloween night. Joined by Dave Alexander on bass, and with Iggy on lead vocals, the band dropped their 'psychedelic' tag, and The Stooges proper were born.

The band lived together from 1967, and became a creative force as well as a stunning local live act. Looking like the Stones, and inspired by the Who, Ravi Shankar, Gregorian chants and Buddhist music, they were among a whole raft of bands looking to extend their R&B chops and find something new, as the 1960s matured from Beatle jackets to beads and kaftans. They played alongside the MC5 many times around Detroit and Michigan, and were jokingly referred to as the MC5's 'little brother band.' Signed by Elektra alongside the MC5, *The Stooges* was released in 1969, and was produced by ex-Velvet Underground's John Cale - a very hip name to have on their first release. Swaggering, malevolent, poppy yet anti-social and wonderful, the band lifted much from the Stones, and with Iggy's increasingly exaggerated delivery on record mirroring his out-of-control stage persona, it is a collection that came as close as any probably could to capturing the nature of the band at the time, leaving the MC5 some way in its wake.

Audiences did not know how to react to The Stooges. In 1969, few of them had witnessed a band whose lead singer would leap into the audience, or would attack the mike stand, instruments or even his own self with such venom. Crowd-surfing is a normal occurrence at even the meekest of rock concerts, but in 1969 an audience was far more likely to part and see Iggy hit the front row of chairs with a crash than to lift him above their heads and pass him around an auditorium.

Gradually the missiles that were hurled at the band from the audience were replaced by plaudits heaped upon them. The Stooges were a band who learned to play on stage, and Iggy was a remarkable sight - muscular, athletic, sexually provocative (he was inspired to 'become' Iggy after witnessing a Doors concert and seeing the wasted sexuality of Jim Morrison at first hand). There's a distinct split between the characters of James Osterberg - the quiet, well-read intellectual whose best friends call him 'Jim' - and Iggy Pop, the peanut-butter-smeared, blood-dripping self-cutter, whose veins stand out on his bare torso as he demands attention, respect and the hearts of every member of an audience.

He often got much more than that, and Stooges gigs could become violent events. Iggy's increasing dependence on drugs pushed his own persona harder and harder as he drew himself to the edge of physical and psychological dissolution. The Stooges were about veracity and commitment. For two years they built a reputation as a live act that few bands have managed to equal: in one sense Iggy created the kind of altered-ego, fucked-up rocker that Bowie's Ziggy Stardust would sharpen into a glitterball of pop a couple of years later, and on the other, gigging harder and louder than anyone, they were a phenomenal touring band.

The improvement was evident in the band's second album, the wonderful *Funhouse,* comprising pretty much the songs that made up the Stooge's live show at the time. Funky, rocky, the album is still a snapshot of a great band on heat, but also a band on the brink of heroin self-destruct. The addition of James Williamson led to a second-phase in the Stooges' brief history. The second guitar player became very close to Iggy, and when Elektra dropped the band due to the hopeless sales of *Funhouse*, the rest of the band felt discarded and surplus to requirements as Pop and Williamson headed for London.

Picked up by David Bowie and introduced to his manager Tony DeFries, Iggy alone was signed to DeFries' Mainman management company. Bowie produced the last Stooges album proper, *Raw Power,* bringing the rest of the band over for sessions and gigs in London, and although many thought that Bowie's production took the balls out of the Stooge's sound, it nevertheless introduced Iggy's band to a new audience of Bowie-philes around the world. An on-off lifetime friendship was formed between Bowie and Pop, and though both would suffer psychological and narcotic excesses in the 1970s, they both produced their most creative work at this period, with Pop's *The Idiot* and *Lust For*

Life being his most successful albums to date (*Raw Power* had, like the previous two albums, stiffed for The Stooges).

For the band, however, time ran out as it had for the MC5. After a disastrous gig at the Michigan Palace Theatre, when a Detroit biker gang fought with the group, Iggy quit. Years before punk, years before new wave, the Ramones, Pearl Jam or Nirvana, The Stooges were *the* nihilistic guitar band. Without Iggy Pop there would have been no Johnny Rotten (himself so clearly an alter-ego for creator John Lydon as Iggy is for James Osterberg), and without The Stooges no Sex Pistols.

A thousand guitar-bands owe their sound - call it grunge, call it punk, call it what you will - to this band who, when most of the rest of the world was skinny-dipping in the waters of the summer of love, foresaw the end of the Woodstock generation before the rest. If the 1960s was defined by Woodstock and ended by Altamont - then the Stooges were a voice marking the transition into the darker, repressive world of the 1970s. More honest than the increasingly ridiculous Doors, less show-biz than the mercurial Stones, perhaps only the Velvet Underground sit alongside The Stooges as signposts to the next generation of guitar bands in both the UK and the States. Literate, sardonic and contrived, the Velvets were the darlings of the New York art set. The Stooges were the darlings of no-one... that is why they are so important.

All this might seem a million miles from The White Stripes, from Meg's pony-tails and Jack's collection of clocks. Not so. Motown, the MC5 and the Stooges run deep in the blood of Detroit. This is not to say they are they key influences on the Stripes – they are categorically not – but they do represent the peak of Detroit's musical personality prior to the Stripes arrival. They are the context, the currency and the oxygen into which The White Stripes were born.

Detroit made practical cars that served ordinary people, and in its entire musical history it could be argued it has produced working, practical music that meets the requirements of ordinary people too. Motown, the MC5 and the Stooges are in a sense practical concepts, just as the blues was a practical way of releasing tension in disenfranchised blacks. The White Stripes fit seamlessly into that vein, nothing is superfluous, everything counts. So even if Jack White doesn't come home and slip a Supremes album into his player, or a live record by the MC5 or Stooges, they are there, watching over his shoulder.

CHAPTER 4

"Rock 'n' roll is a communicable disease."

The New York Times, 1956.

While still working for Muldoon's furniture business, Jack successfully auditioned for the drummer's position in an established local band called Goober And The Peas. This outfit was deep into country territory although this was spliced with lashings of punk, an odd mix but nonetheless one which made a significant impact on Jack - his blues leanings have always erred more towards country blues than any other splinter group within that genre. During his stint in this band, he was always listed as Jack 'Doc' Gillis - using his real surname and the band's generic nickname (a twist of the Ramones shared moniker) Goober And The Peas released several albums throughout the early 1990s with various line-ups.

One of the aspects of this five-piece band which Jack found particularly frustrating was how that rigidity of format restricted him from changing songs at each gig. Later, with The White Stripes, he would be able to alter tracks every single night if he so wished - and he frequently does - but here he was necessarily confined to what the five-piece could do.

In one of the rare insights into Jack's formative musical years, a superb article by Brian McCollum in *The Detroit Free Press* revealed much about Jack's motivations at this stage. Dan Miller, singer and guitarist with Goober had this to say about him: "We knew we'd be touring a lot, so we wanted someone whose personality we liked, too. Jack was a lot younger than we were. He wasn't the most technical drummer, thankfully - not a Neil Peart-ish drummer. Everybody in the band was like, 'Wow!' It was great to see somebody with that kind of passion for music. His instincts were really great… I think it was a good thing for him just to see what it was like to be in a band that toured - and probably see what kind of mistakes we made. I do remember the first show when he played drums: for an encore he came up and sang some Elvis song. People where just shocked by his passion for it."

Miller went on to tell McCollum, "It was weird, knowing him at nineteen, and seeing this person who had all these really clear-cut goals and this real commitment and passion for how he wanted things to go in his life, musically and otherwise. I remember him saying, 'I really want to be proud of everything I do.'"

Miller's own stage presence would have a lasting effect on Jack, as during this time he started to present himself in a more considered way and was obviously becoming more aware of image and style. It was also during this stint as Goober's sticksman that Jack is said to have first met Meg, who was still living on the east side of town. She was a very shy girl, he was more outgoing, with a shock of blond, curly hair. They quickly began dating and became very close, sharing a passion for old vinyl and increasingly obscure musical reference points. They married in 1996, and Jack took Meg's surname.

With Jack and Meg about to embark on their career in The White Stripes – and with Jack keeping himself busy with numerous other projects too - it is worth looking at what was happening in Detroit's music circles in prior to this. There were two key aspects to chronicle. Firstly, perhaps the single most influential Detroit band of this modern era – albeit posthumously – the Gories. And secondly, the beginning of the genesis of the scene that would eventually led to the Stripes, but which started off with bands such as Rocket 455 and the Hentchmen, and later Outrageous Cherry.

With comments associating The White Stripes with artists such as Hendrix, Zeppelin and the Yardbirds, it is easy for music historians to have a field day conjecturing about the key influences on Jack and Meg in their formative years. Yet for Jack's part, he has offered up far more colloquial idols, in particular the Gories, who had an enormous mark on Jack but have also been credited with starting the entire Detroit rock scene of the late 1990s.

The man at the centre of the Gories is Mick Collins. I spoke with him at length about the band he formed and the musical choices he made which later had such a profound effect on Jack White. To understand Mick's view on music is to simultaneously enlighten yourself on Jack's.

Mick was born in 1965 and brought up in Detroit. "Music was always around, we had a ton of records in our basement. My dad worked across the street from the States' largest record distributor. I was the youngest of six kids by ten years, so my siblings were all kids at the beginning of rock 'n' roll. This distributor would always give my dad a couple of records off the top of the box, so we had a fairly complete history of rock 'n' roll from when I was a kid. Thousands of old 45s, blues, everything. One of the first records I owned was 'Good Golly Miss Molly' by Little Richard. Yet I am the only one in my entire extended family on both sides with any career in the arts and we are talking seventy people on each side. I got made fun of by everybody!

I missed all the Beatles, the Stooges all of that. As a kid I just liked what was on the radio. Everyone makes out all these references for Detroit music but I was listening to stuff like Curtis Mayfield, Barry White, the O' Jays and 1970s soul essentially. I got into punk rock one day when I was flipping the radio around out of boredom. I decided to start at one end of the dial and work my way to the other end until I found something interesting. Over a two-week period, I worked my way through all these stations. This particular Friday in 1980, I was flipping on to the next station and turned it to a radio playing 'Gates Of Steel' by Devo, so I kept listening. It was the only punk rock radio show in town and even then was on air for only two hours. But punk was only one of my influences, probably not even a major one. I did, however, become a huge Residents fan, I loved their noise.

My first band that left any trace was the Floor Tasters. There was an obscure recording by a performance artist called 'I Taste Floor' and I thought that was the best title ever. We were mostly influenced by Wire."

The Gories have been held up as pretty much the only band of substance in Detroit in the late 1980s, typifying the fact there was no real music scene to speak of. Mick categorically disagrees: "There were *dozens* of bands in town, it was just that nobody was taking any notice of them. There have always been tons of bands in Detroit. There was a record label called Tremor which did the more interesting local bands, there were 45s and some groups did their own. For example, there was a band called Society that was weird and very noisy. Radio was there too. If a band sent a radio station a tape it would get played. It was more that there was no media focus rather than no music. That held true right up to the recent media attention (of the late 1990s).

A year after The Floor Tasters, came The Gories, which formed in 1986. "I went with some friends to a gig and saw this guy with a pink English Beat T-shirt. I had to find out where this guy got this T-shirt from - we were Mods at the time. I asked this guy and he was so flipped out that this black guy wanted to know about the English Beat. This was Tom Lynch and he introduced me to Dan (Kroha – founding member of The Gories), who actually lived near to me. We've been friends ever since.

I used to DJ at Mod parties where Dan would play and at one of these events we met Peggy O'Neill. A year or so later Dan and Peg became an item and another month later all three of us formed The Gories. We called our friend Fred to play drums but he wasn't home so Dan said Peg should do it. She had never played drums before – mind you, I was a drummer not a bassist!

Myself and Dan were sitting around drinking beer, listening to a compilation called *The Scum Of The Earth* and we said, 'You know, we can play better than this and we can't even play!' That was our motivation to form the band. Simple as that.

Much has been made of comparisons with The White Stripes in that some reports had The Gories was always a bassless act. Wrong again says Mick. "It is absolutely not true that we had no bass. I was originally the bassist but the problem was that Dan couldn't solo on guitar, he could hold the chords down well but not solo. I couldn't play solo but I could play single notes. So we decided to switch when needed. We went out and bought a bass but it became too big a hassle to keep switching, so that is how that happened. Simple as that. It was pure pragmatism. Having said that, we never actually played any gigs with a bass, yet we do get mail occasionally saying there is a bass there but there wasn't. That was only in rehearsal.

After eight months we played our first gig at the St Andrews Church for a community series in the September of 1986. We were Mods and we wanted to play R&B and Chess blues. Garage rock was petering out - the real garage revival scene as I see it - had come and gone by 1986. We would get these Mod fanzines and read these reviews of bands that said they were "wild and primitive" but when we heard them we would think, "That's not wild and primitive, that's jangly pop!" So we said we would be the most amped-up, fuzzed out, noisey, punk R&B band that all these other acts claimed to be but never actually were.

Much has also been made of how the Gories chose to have no bass out of some deep, primal musical motivation and how they played the blues because it was the most honest and soulful music of all – hence the appeal of the Gories to Jack White. Mick has a rather more honest (and modest?) suggestion: "Although we were Mods it was the 1960s soul, especially Chess Blues and R&B that was more of an influence on the Gories. We were not that accomplished at that stage and we worked out that if a song had more than six notes we couldn't play it. So we had to strip everything down to that number of notes. We just couldn't play! That may debunk another myth about us but that is the simple truth. We would literally have to count the notes - 'You Don't Love Me' by Bo Diddley has three notes so that was in! When we got better, nine notes was our absolute limit.

35

Like the Stripes, The Gories gigged *hard*. "Our very first show was supported by the MC5's Rob Tyner who played two hours of folk songs on auto-harp. We played everywhere. In 1987 we played every other week, usually to eight or ten people opening for other bands in town. We didn't headline shows in Detroit until our final year, the end of 1991. There never was any momentum behind the band - it was the same thirty people who would show up at every show. Every so often we will meet people who say, 'Hey, I used to see you guys all the time.' We'd be like, 'I don't know you!' If you came to a Gories show in the late 1980s we would know you!"

Yet out of town, Gories' shows were getting big. "We did a show in Hoboken and as we approached the club there was this huge line of people around the block, a completely sold-out show. They were there to see us and we couldn't believe it. Yet in Detroit we were just another band. The media says in 1989 there was only The Gories Detroit, but there were hundreds of bands, you could see a different band every night of the week. For example, there was a psychedelic punk band called the Hysteric Narcotics who we supported all the time. We were not the headlining act in Detroit.

While Mick plays down the band's influence with admirable modesty, there is no doubt that they developed a sizeable following, albeit predominantly abroad and outside of Detroit. Ironically, it was on a European tour that the band came to a premature end – sad considering they were one of the very first of this new generation of Detroit acts to tour the Continent. "We were on Crypt Records from New Jersey and the owner of the label moved to Germany and that's how we got that European tour, lucky really. Along with Chess Blues, his *Back From The Grave* compilations were the biggest influence on the Gories. The Gories finished because we couldn't stand each other anymore. It wasn't musical differences, that was the least of it. We had that disastrous European tour and it was like, 'Don't call me!'"

Mick went on to form a new band called the Dirtbombs in 1992, although he first played in the King Sound Quartet and then the Screws for a short while. It was, however, the Dirtbombs who would become Mick's longest project of all.

Since the demise of The Gories, they have passed into Detroit legend as the single most important band of the late 1980s and early 1990s. Jack White is frequently heard singing their praises. All this acclaim comes as some surprise to Mick. "It makes me chuckle, it amuses me when I read about the Gories. The band broke up in 1992, and suddenly [after the White Stripes breakthrough] everyone wants to talk to us. I am reading everywhere that *Houserockin'* was the start of so much for this latest generation of garage rock, yet when we were doing that, that record pretty much hacked off the garage rock revival, it had all petered out by 1989 when that was released. We never saw ourselves as the beginning of anything. I'm told all the time that we appealed to a lot of people but we never knew about that, we never knew anyone was listening to the records, we were just happy to have them out. It wasn't until years later that we heard these things being said."

NME called the Gories "the band who effectively triggered the Detroit rock renaissance. "I am not sure I can buy into that. We were reviled around town, not least because we were so bad. To say we had a negligible effect on the town would be an overstatement. We were voted worst band in town two years in a row! On the one hand, it is gratifying to hear all these complementary things said about The Gories but on the other hand, where the hell were all these people when it mattered! No one cared when we were there and no one cared when we left. Bands that came after us were listening to anything but The Gories. I think it is almost like we have been elevated to the level of myth like the MC5 and the Stooges. No other Gories-like bands sprang up in the wake of The Gories. I can't believe that we had any sort of lasting influence on Detroit rock, I do appreciate those things being said but it is laughable man!"

Despite this, Jack White is in no doubt about Mick's band's importance to him. Unlike many scenesters, Jack's involvement with The Gories came while that band were still in existence, as Mick explains. "My first experience of Jack was when he came by the house to drop off something. I found out later he had driven the entire length of this eight mile road in one go, using only the street on which I live. Yet it is crossed by freeways and all sorts of roads, it is impossible to get here in a straight line, so I have no idea how he managed to do that, and I can't imagine what he saw on his way! I don't know why he did that. At that point, he was just another guy in a band.

The second time I met him was much later, The White Stripes were opening for the Dirtbombs. All I remember is being at the bar then I don't remember much after that. I got rip-roaring drunk before they went on. It was still daylight outside when they went on, I recall that much but nothing else."

Mick has this to say about Jack's apparent obsession with The Gories. "I can't honestly say I remember seeing him, but everyone says he is a Gories fan. To be fair, we didn't know absolutely everybody, lots of them never came back!"

As for any direct similarities between The White Stripes and The Gories, Mick is reserved. "I think the Gories were a lot more punk and blues-based. To be utterly honest, the stylistic similarities are there to a degree but the difference is that The Gories were more urban blues-based whereas the White Stripes are more country blues-based. We did do Leadbelly songs and things like that but in terms of the actual music, the make-up of that, our influence was electric blues whereas the Stripes was more country blues. But yes, we are both blues-based and playing rock music. That is probably the closest similarity but it is also a big difference."

Speaking of The White Stripes decision from day one not to have a bass guitar, Mick has this to say. "People say 'but The Gories had no bass', but Jack was in other bands that had bass guitars in there also. Besides it wasn't just the Gories, although from Detroit we were the only band without a bass. Cheater Slicks also don't have a bass player. We knew of others from out of town. Dejavoodoo out of Montreal were the very first of the guitar and drum duos and we all knew about them living on the border with Canada so they were always on the radio. A person could probably make the argument that White Stripes were more influenced by Dejavoodoo than The Gories.

Other Detroit rock luminaries are certain Mick's band was pivotal in Jack's formation of The White Stripes. Jim Diamond produced The White stripes' first two album and is the city's most prominent rock studio wizard. He had this to say to me about The Gories: "The biggest influence [on Jack] would definitely be the Gories. In terms of the rawness and the sound of it. The Gories were just doing stripped down blues music, R&B and distorted electric guitars. Mick is black so it's that strange old story where the white artist imitates the black artist and on it goes from there. So Mick was doing that stripped down blues music years earlier, as far back as 1989."

Although Mick seems unaware of the impact his band had on Jack, White's cousin Ben was more clear when I asked him about this: "Jack really looks up to The Gories. He bought a record one day in a store and Mick was behind him in line. And Jack was all excited... 'Mick Collins was just behind me in line!'"

38

For his part, Jack had this to say: "I'd say The Gories pretty much sums up the feel of Detroit. That to me feels like Detroit. I know there's an image to what Detroit is around the nation probably, and it's not like a huge ghetto, but it's not like a modern city either. Especially their second album, *I Know You Fine, But How You Doin'*, that's like real Detroit to me."

After the Gories came a small cluster of bands who were largely on their own in the scene for some time. Rocket 455, the Hentchmen and Outrageous Cherry were probably at the core. Matt Smith of the latter was inspired to start playing by a lone Detroit pseudo-punk hit. "The Romantics were Detroit's answer to the Sex Pistols – that's how someone once put it. I was a kid playing these clubs and getting thrown out of the clubs with my equipment still on stage for not having the proper ID. Then in the 1980s I played in various groups when I was in college and then when I got out of school I went to film school and graduated but found I didn't have the money to make film. So I started playing rock 'n' roll and haven't really stopped since.

Outrageous Cherry started in 1992/3 and there was no scene to play. I didn't even know why I started a band. The bands that we used to play with at that time – there was literally only an audience of twenty people, it was us, Rocket 455, the Demolition Dollar, the Hentchmen and that's it. I don't really remember anything else. There was an Ann Arbour band called Coach that was amazing. Dan Kroha from the Gories was in two of these bands (The Doll Rods and Rocket). At one show I singing on stage with Mick Collins, sort of screaming with Mick next to me smashing records with power tools. I don't know exactly how I got on stage."

John Szymanski of the Hentchmen is another classic example of a Detroit band member. His first band was a ska outfit called the Exceptions in the late 1980s, who even played one gig with the Gories. He told me how, "It was punk rock and the Specials – we thought that was great. However, it was real short lived, we just formed the band for parties and play at house parties (many of which were in Ann Arbour, again to be mentioned later).

We didn't know there was actually a scene to speak of in Detroit for some time. Plus the scene that I was kinda hanging out with didn't even care that much for the Stooges and MC5. We were more into authentic 1960s stuff. We started the Hentchmen in 1992 and it didn't take too long before we put some singles out - Norton Records in New York liked our demo. They signed us up for a few albums so we just made a load of trashy basement recordings, really crude stuff. The first half of our back-catalogue is just four track recordings that were fun at the time.

In the mid-1990s, Asterisk Records were doing small festivals to about 500 people around the North West - there might be a couple of New York bands, a couple of Florida bands whatever, but we kind of got lumped in with that scene. We did some singles with small labels around America.

This story is typical of how hard working many of these key Detroit bands are – and explains why they find it so amusing when, post-White Stripes, the media talk of them being the "latest hot bands". The Hentchmen were playing Detroit about once a month at this point, "because those shows were not as much fun, people in Detroit were always hard to get out. They were stay-at-homes. That's why a lot of bands that come to town have a hard time getting an audience."

The Hentchmen, like Outrageous Cherry and Rocket 455, persevered and went on to establish themselves as founders – behind the Gories – of the current crop of bands. Without these acts, there probably would be no White Stripes.

CHAPTER 5

" 'Shit or get off the pot Seger! No cry babies allowed in rock 'n'
roll!' I never got better advice."

Bob Seger recalling words of wisdom from Ted Nugent during his early performing days, 1983.

Meanwhile, Jack's prolific association with numerous bands continued.
After leaving Goober And The Peas, he joined an act called Two Star
Tabernacle, who played a conglomeration of country, blues and rock,
again also featuring Dan Miller (from Goober), Miller's wife Tracee and
drummer Damian Lang. Jack first played with Two Star Tabernacle in
early 1997, only a few months before the newly-formed White Stripes
played their first ever gig.

Having been at the very heart of the emerging Detroit scene since
day one, Jeff Meier of Rocket 455 (also briefly of the Detroit Cobras and
the Hentchmen) knew pretty much everyone there was to know. His first
experience of Jack White was at a most unusual location. "I read in the
paper that Kitty Wells was playing, the old country singer - her husband
was real popular too in country music in the 1950's. And she can make
honky tonk boom! Oddly though, she was playing in the Senior Citizens
Centre, this little centre in the middle of a suburban neighbourhood.

I like all kinds of music and through my dad got exposed to country.
I couldn't believe it - Kitty Wells, when was I ever going to see her in
Detroit again? Maybe in Nashville perhaps, but coming to this little dinky
place way out in New Pontiac? It was really strange. So I eagerly drove
out to the gig where I found a big tour bus outside the Centre, treating
them like rock stars! There were about five people who were under sixty
five. One of those was Jack White.

After this peculiar first meeting, Jack and Jeff saw each other around
quite often. By this time, Jack had gained enough experience at the craft
of upholstery to strike out on his own (later, when Jack had already
graced the covers of dozens of magazines as the Stripes went global, he
went for dinner with local record label owner Dave Buick and, noticing a
hole in the latter's sofa, ran home, returned with some tools and repaired
it).

"A friend of mine owned a building," continues Jeff Meier, "and
had turned it into artists' studios. Jack was renting one of them to run

his own upholstery business from, so I'd see him there. He was doing music of course, but he couldn't play in this building itself because they didn't allow rock 'n' roll or anything to be practised or whatever. It was supposed to be for artists." This little studio had a guitar in it, some sewing machines, chairs and some artwork, sculptures and wall hangings.

"I'd go over to his upholstery shop," recalls Jeff, "and we'd listen to music or whatever and shoot the shit, you know. I remember he was really rapt about Bob Dylan and the Flat Duo Jets. They were like his favourites when we were hanging out. He even upholstered my kitchen chairs - that I'm sitting on right now - and you know what colour they are too!"

It was around this time that Jack first started jamming with his wife Meg. The story goes that Jack was fiddling around practising his guitar and Meg just decided to sit herself behind his drum kit. Within minutes they were jamming a rudimentary version of Bowie's 'Moonage Daydream'. Jack – used to the confines of four and five piece bands - immediately saw the potential of this set-up, as he told *Q* magazine. "Playing with another guy always leads into competitiveness. With Meg there was a different approach. She played drums in a whole new way. She wasn't trying to be loud or complex… and there was no clash of egos. What she did was just so simple, basic and uncluttered, which was so refreshing."

Having successfully convinced an initially reluctant Meg to play the drums, Jack named his new band after something very simple: striped peppermint candy. This was a very blunt symbol of the White Stripes whole ethos towards their music. "Anyone else would be excess. It would defeat the purpose of centralizing on these three components of storytelling, melody and rhythm." They also vowed to wear only red and white on stage too, because "it stands out and will maybe help people remember us better." Black was also occasionally used - the strongest colour combination in alchemy and most of the West's magical systems, as well as in voodoo.

Jack's cousin, Ben Blackwell later told Brian McCollum that, "When I first heard about them naming the band the White Stripes, I thought people were going to think they were a skinhead band. Originally they were tossing back and forth the names Bazooka and Soda Powder, so after hearing the other names they had come up with, The White Stripes didn't seem so bad. Meg came up with it, and the story about them getting it from the candy might be true, but they also had some old bricks in front of the house in the garden that said 'White' on them, and that might have had something to do with it." At this point, however, this was all conjecture - as yet, The White Stripes had played no gigs and had no songs.

Two Star Tabernacle produced only one record, a seven inch cover of Hank Williams' 'Ramblin' Man', which featured veteran R&B vocalist Andre Williams. It was produced by Jeff Meier, from the aforementioned Rocket 455, one of the veterans of the Detroit scene.

Jeff spoke with me at length about these sessions for Jack White, some of The White Stripes' man's earliest dealings with recording equipment. "I thought Jack was getting right on down with Andre straight away in the sessions. He was pretty much trying to sell Andre (a song called that he had written called) 'The Big Three Killed My Baby'. But it wasn't going to happen, Andre had in his mind what he was going to do. Everybody who was involved was somewhat overwhelmed because Andre Williams was one of our heroes, he had this mystique. Here I was getting to record him! We just used my portable studio, I took all my gear over to Jack's house in the Mexican quarter. I thought the house was pretty weird, you know, but kinda cool.

At this point, it seems that Jack's much mooted encyclopaedic knowledge of music history was not yet apparent: "He wasn't into anything off the wall. He liked Love quite a bit but had a standard record collection [Author's Note: something which Jack himself admits]. He didn't have a whole lot of records - maybe about thirty or forty. When I first met him, he was really into two things, Love and Dylan. The irony was I'm pretty sure he'd never heard Andre Williams before he played with him.

I was actually quite reluctant to accept the job because there wasn't a whole lot of money involved. I had to take a day off work to do it - I was working as a technician in an electronic shop at the time but that didn't pay the bills. They convinced me because of Andre Williams being involved, plus Andre really wanted me to do it. We've always gotten along good and enjoyed a big mutual respect for each other.

Even when I'd got everything set up, they didn't know what songs they were going to record. It was chaotic. Problem was it took a couple of hours just to get set up. I think it took all day to do two songs, even though we got there pretty early to set up. Having said all that, I kinda liked doing it that way. There was the drum set up in the dining room - a good separation for the sound. The piano was set up in this big living room/dining room in the corner of the house. It was just a big open area so I could place things where I wanted. That's why it sounded good you know. (Noise) wasn't bleeding over into every other track. A little bit of bleed always makes a recording sound natural, of course, but I didn't want it to be out of control where I couldn't do a good mix of it later."

Jeff was impressed both with Jack's technical ability and his application: "I thought he had real interesting guitar parts throughout. Plus he had this high voice, there were some really cool and high harmonies in there. As far as that session goes, in the end I don't think they actually did anything that Jack wanted to do with Andre. He spent a lot of time trying to convince them to do that one song but they ended up not doing it. He's with this old R&B soul singer and wants to record 'The Big Three Killed My Baby'! It was worth a try and I admire him for being persistent! That's the kinda guy Jack is - he doesn't take no for an answer - although he had to that day…"

To this day, Jeff vividly recalls Jack's focus, even at such an early stage: "I thought he was much more driven than anybody I'd ever known. Certain other people were driven but they weren't surrounding themselves with all the right people like Jack was. He had a knack for knowing about, and placing himself in, good situations. All these projects that he did, like Two Star and the [later] recordings with the Hentchmen were very well chosen. These bands were underground, really respected and had real integrity. These sort of musicians would never kowtow to any trend, they're just really into what they're doing.

Jack placed himself in among those people and at the time this gave him a lot of credibility - he was after all a nobody trying to make it. Even tougher was the fact that he was trying to go from the coffee house scene into the rock 'n' roll scene. And I think he did what he had to do…"

What Jeff is referring to by "the coffee house scene" was something which Jack had been involved in around Detroit in order to gain live experience and work his way through his own songs and ideas. Much of Jack and Meg's very early experience in the Detroit world came within this low-key scene. This is where Jeff Meier of Rocket 455 saw Jack perform first. "He was playing at a place called Planet Ant. Cheesy, underage, arty. Because of the drinking age in America, all the kids who were under twenty-one go for a drink in these coffee houses. It's a real hit or miss as far as the music they put on is concerned - mostly miss, acoustic, introspective, sensitive stuff.

When I started in music, the coffee house thing didn't really exist to that degree, but throughout the 1990s it caught on real big. Every little neighbourhood had a place where all these kids could hang out. I never had that. I'd always sneak in somewhere through backdoor...

Jack played at a lot of these places. I don't know if anyone really gave a shit if he had or not, but I think on his own personal level he wanted to surround himself with people that he looked up to in rock 'n' roll circles, rather than within the coffee house circuit."

Jeff was not the only person who began to see something extra in the aspiring work of the young Jack White. Aforementioned Detroit producer Jim Diamond's first meeting with Jack was playing with Two Star Tabernacle, although he said "I never really liked that band."

As probably the key journalist on the emerging scene, Gary Graff could also see from his perspective that Jack was no ordinary band member. "He was known but there was no real diva attitude there. People knew him as a really good kid, an interesting guy but I always felt there was a sense that he was a visionary and marched to the beat of his own drum. He was clearly a very distinctive individual with a talented personality."

It was the summer of 1997. Jack was spending increasing amounts of his time and ideas on his duo with Meg, The White Stripes. It was time to play their first show. The question was – where would they play it?

The so-called 'Cass Corridor' in Detroit is a stretch of urban grubbiness and social deprivation, stuck between the north shadow of the city's skyline and Wayne State University. It is home to countless seedy bars, prostitution and the homeless... and probably the single most important venue at the heart of Detroit's resurgent garage rock scene, The Gold Dollar. The White Stripes played here countless times, as did almost every major band in the area. Before The Gold Dollar, there was a small coffee bar in Cass Corridor called Zoot's, which was reputedly an ex-whorehouse where some bands would play, including the Wildbunch who became Electric Six. Mick Collins of The Gories fame even played there with Matt Smith of Outrageous Cherry in a project called Yeti Sanction.

However, it was The Gold Dollar was that central to this latest generation of Detroit rockers. The enigmatic character behind this locally legendary venue is Neil Yee, a Colorado-native. I spoke with Neil Yee about his motivations and ambitions when running The Gold Dollar. In light of the corporate attempts to hijack the Detroit 'scene' for commercial gain, what is intriguing and refreshing about speaking to

Yee is the completely engaging way he relates the story and the apparent absence of any commercial or corporate mentality, an attitude that was perhaps so central to the success of his club. His reasons for opening this venue provide some of the most fascinating vignettes in all the many varied and colourful stories behind the explosion of music in Detroit in the mid-to-late-1990s.

"From 1987 to 1990, I went to college in Wisconsin because I could get to play hockey at weekends. I wasn't really very serious about my education but nevertheless I paid my way through college doing sound for bands in Madison and I had a great time. There was some really good music around there then - at the time, Butch Vig was running a little studio, there was the band Swamp Thing, it was a really good scene. I originally wanted to work with video but I then decided I was more into the live scene. I kept with my education up specifically to get a job to make some money to open a venue up. In 1990, I moved to Detroit and got a corporate job."

So many people have dreamed of owning their own music venue. Yee, undeterred by the costs, the risks and his relative youthfulness (he was only in his early twenties when he opened The Gold Dollar) was always going to realise that dream: "It was one of those things where I just couldn't figure out what else I wanted. I'd always wanted to do something like that, the time seemed right and I didn't have much else going on. Then again, I always think I don't have much going on but I'm always doing about twenty things at once!

At that point in time, I'd put some money together which allowed me three options; I was either going to go to graduate school; or I was going to just take off and paddle around the world for a year or two; or open a venue. I thought the last option was the highest risk. I just thought, 'I can go to school later, I can travel later. I think I'm only crazy enough to try this right now.' I just really enjoy live music and I was going to gigs all the time, so I thought it would be interesting to try. I didn't really know what I was doing."

His strategy to find the right venue and at the right price was ingenious: "By 2002, everything had picked up in Detroit and everyone was trying to sell buildings for a lot of money - but when I first starting looking for a building in 1994, I would drive to the city and find something that I thought - from the outside - might work. Then I'd go into the city offices and look up the tax records. If that building was behind with the taxes by a decent amount, it meant that the person didn't care about it a whole lot, so I would write to the tax address saying I was interested in buying the building, knowing that I would have to pay off the back taxes. That is what I did with the building that eventually became The Gold Dollar - I spotted it in late 1994 and, this time, I got a response from the owner who was living in Alabama.

The empty building I bought had been closed since 1989. The old sign on the front said 'Cartel Lounge', but it was called The Gold Dollar from 1935 through 1988 when it was a bar. From the 1950s through 1987, it was a drag show bar. I really couldn't come up with any alternative names for the place and when I was mentioned Cartel Lounge to people, everyone kept saying, 'Oh, that's the old Gold Dollar isn't it?' It was rather infamous with the police too, so I thought I'd go with that name because you can't argue with history. When we first opened, I got a lot of great stories from old regulars coming in and the occasional drag queen who hadn't been in town in twenty years saying, 'I can't believe this place is still open.'

I got a letter of authority to have a locksmith open up the building. I went in, took a look around and decided to buy it. It was very dumpy inside, people had been living in the back room and it was a mess. Drug users and stuff, but I figured it was salvageable. When they closed the venue the last time, they obviously hadn't cleaned up, they'd just had their last party there and you could still see the aftermath.

I bought the interest in January 1995 and we worked on it all year ready to open in 1996. We had to do a lot of work cleaning it up. I wasn't working on it constantly, it was just me and whatever friends felt like doing something at weekends. I still had a full time job. For a while, it didn't appear that it was going to open at all, because it needed a lot of work and, as I say, I was just financing it off of my day job.

There were always people offering to do things - when we were getting closer to opening and people phoned to hang out or do something, I'd be like, 'Well, I was going to work on the building. Why don't you come by, have a couple of beers and work on the building with me?' I remember a second date with a girl called Cindy was spent painting the logo outside. We cut out these templates and she was standing up this ladder and all these guys were walking by saying things - but she did a great job and we're still friends. That's what you remembered from a date with Neil Yee was, not the sex but painting the building!"

Despite his best intentions, Neil never quite finished the full refurbishment of the run-down building. He had a liquor licence with an expiry date and needed insurance regardless of whether he was open or not "I thought, 'I might as well open'. So, I was planning on fixing it up a little bit more but then by the time we were operating and I had the money to do all the other things that I had originally wanted to do, it didn't seem worth it because the venue was already working well the way that it was. Why bother remodelling when it's already working?"

Befitting this very practical approach, The Gold Dollar on opening night was a very simple venue. "How it looked when we were finally ready to open for business didn't change the whole time it was open. The main room had this old red carpet down and was probably forty feet by about twenty or thirty feet, pretty small. When you first walked in the building, the stage was on the right and to the left was the bar, which ran the full length of the room. The stage was eleven feet deep and seventeen feet wide, which took up a good proportion of the room, kinda in the middle of the long side of the room, rather than at one end which is more the norm. That layout wasn't ideal for sound, but it was ideal for paying attention to the band! Also, other venues often had a back room where everyone could disappear, but The Gold Dollar was unique in that there was way to escape the band! You were always near by, you could only stand either at the side of the stage or right in front. That was about it. You could not get more than twenty feet or so away from the performers. If you decided you wanted to have a conversation - you couldn't! I saw it as a performance venue not as a bar. Besides, although it wasn't ideal in a lot of ways, but by the time I actually got the money to change it, I kind of got to like that arrangement."

This unorthodox layout did present certain audio challenges for Neil, who ran the sound desk himself. "The difficulty with a wide stage like that is things sounded great if you're standing near the edge of the stage, but if you're right up front and centre you're kind of in between the speakers and almost behind them. It depended where you were in the room as to how it sounded, particularly if the band was way too loud. On most nights, the worst sound was right in front of the stage in the centre!"

Just as Neil refurbished the venue largely on his own and with friends, his approach to the equipment carried a similar DIY ethic. "A lot of the stuff I had left over from doing sound for other bands. I'd bought some used equipment and some new cabinets but rebuilt all of them, so the final result was basically a home-built system. The monitors were particularly home-built and they usually would work, although not always! The desk had eight channels and a eight channel cassette recording system that I had wired in there and I typically didn't use more than eight microphones. I have some really good live recordings of quite a bit of the stuff that went on there, including White Stripes shows.

The bar was there on the wall directly opposite the stage. I figured to run the bar to pay for the all the crazy things I wanted to do there." By that, Neil is referring to the famously peculiar and seemingly incongruous bills that he put on - deliberately. "It's funny because what The Gold Dollar is known for most of all is The White Stripes - the whole garage rock thing. However, what I really wanted to do was a lot more experimental stuff that no one else would book and that didn't really make any money. Experimental noise bands, acts that no one was going near at the time but my motivation was that I wanted to be able to experience new music."

Neil did the sound and sometimes the door, although he rarely tended the bar ("I was terrible!"); "Our main bar person - the one who was there the longest was Amy Abbott - who was known to show up in strange costumes and wigs. She became a known personality around town. Before that was Heather White, Meg's sister, for a year or so, and Leah Smith for the first few months. I'd say almost all the staff were in bands or were artists of one kind or another. Quite an eclectic and interesting crew. Some might go so far as to say freak show!"

Jack White himself played a part in the exterior decoration: "The sign outside was just thrown together. It's not a very good design piece... it's amazing it stayed as long as it did. One of my room-mates at the time had come up with something for the sign but I thought it was absolutely terrible. So I went onto the computer at work and tried to learn how to use the graphics software. About an hour and a half later, I came up with the sign we used. It was meant to be temporary but, like a lot of things in that business, we never quite got around to doing anything else. Jack White offered to carve the sign in wood for when we first opened."

That very first night when The Gold Dollar opened is ingrained in Neil's memory. "I think we were trying to be a little bit weirder than everyone was ready for. There was a band called Twitch that I liked even though they weren't popular with the garage rock scene. They were like King Crimson doing comedy and novelty songs. They were incredible musicians playing these goofy songs so I made them the headline act of the opening night. Before them I had my friend Alan Franklin who was in a number of bands playing just acoustic guitar. Opening the bill, we had an original play called *The Red Geraniums* written by my friend Indi and I (actually she wrote most of it!).

It was a great night, we did well that night. It was definitely sold out. Our legal capacity was 107. Typically we would cut it off at about 150 and at that point you really can't move. And that night we had that. I should have made more of the opening night but I barely had enough money to get the place open. I'd done a trial run the night before when one of my bands played. I invited people I knew from the neighbourhood and a lot of friends but we had to tell people to 'quit buying the American beers, the Budweiser and stuff because we're going to run out for opening night tomorrow.' We wanted to have a good selection of beers and I didn't have the money to buy more than a case or two of anything, so that first night we ran out of nearly everything. But because I had a full time job anyway for most of the time I was running it, I didn't really need to make any money out of it."

Unfortunately, Neil's eclectic tastes did not always meet with mass approval. "We tried running the play before the bands for a month there. But it didn't really work. We did some other original theatre later on but that didn't really work too well either. I liked the idea of booking things that don't go together well. I enjoyed the variety. We used to book some really punk bands and put a magician in between them just for fun. A lot of things just didn't work, and that's perhaps one of the reasons why I (eventually) got tired of running the place because I figured out what worked. And I think the fun for me was experimenting and making people sit through something that they really didn't want to. We had all kinds of really weird things going on there that were not expected and people would show up on the wrong night and would be expecting some punk rock band and they'd end up with some 70-year-old guy playing flamenco. We only had about five regulars who would come to all the oddities that we would have regardless. Some of the off-the-wall bookings were huge and some of them nobody showed up. We were known for doing these horribly inconsistent shows."

Neil's personalised approach was even more impressive for the fact that he was not involved for the inevitable cool cliques that most scenes have. "I would never hang out with the people in the scene and that kind of thing. I just did what I was doing - everybody else would go to the after-show party and I would just go home. I was kind of anti-social. When I later saw The White Stripes at the Masonic Temple in 2003, I went with Heather and her mum. We went back stage and everyone was really surprised to see me because I rarely go out or do anything. I just did my thing and that was all I wanted to do."

For the bands that would go on to make this venue the very heart of the Detroit scene, Neil's openness about the finances was a key attraction. "I wanted to set up a venue that was run like the places I liked to play, where they were honest with bands about the money. We gave everyone 100% of the door - we never held back money out for sound or whatever, it was always 100% for the band. Also, hardly anyone got in for free, even friends, we were like, 'it doesn't matter - the money goes to the band'. There was one of the local papers that didn't like us because we wouldn't advertise with them and we always charged their people when they came in. Then they said they would not write any reviews of our shows and, I said, 'I don't really care. It's kind of fine as it is.' There was a certain level of arrogance that went along with it - but at least we were honest. Sometimes, the band would get more than the door, if we put up a guaranteed fee that was too high and didn't collect much at the door, but the band would still get paid."

People other than Neil Yee urged me to interview him and chronicle this venue for this book. As mentioned above, The Gold Dollar was in one of the most singularly uninviting neighbourhoods in Detroit, hidden away in the old, run-down Chinatown, a totally unlikely quarter of town to start a new business. It was a predominantly black area and suffered extreme inner city deprivation. "It was a very transient neighbourhood," Jeff Meier told me. "There were prostitutes everywhere, a lot of crack and heroin. It was probably about the poorest area in town really. Real seedy. Beyond anything I could really explain. Perhaps every third time there was a show something would happen to someone. One night, I was sitting out front before we played and I saw some guy walking down the street on the other side just busting out every single car window as he walked by. I think some of the neighbourhood people were not pleased that there were so many white kids coming from the suburbs hanging out. Once Neil Yee convinced people that they weren't going to get killed when they went to The Gold Dollar, all the bands wanted to play there."

The Gold Dollar was open three or four night a week. The only other major venue for these bands was excellent The Magic Stick, which was also a very major part of this scene. However, according to many of the musicians I have interviewed for this book, that venue had a much bigger central room and as such the intimacy and character of The Gold Dollar seemed to attract the most attention.

Andy, owner of the Detroit label Flying Bomb (that would later put out a White Stripes Christmas single) speculates that it wasn't just the style and size of The Gold Dollar which made it so appealing. "You knew that the bands playing would get the money from the door," he told me. "You knew there were no promoters or other people involved. That was great."

The venue was small, very small. "If you had 200 people in there you thought you were going to die!" recalls Jim Diamond, whose very first experience of The White Stripes - like many people in Detroit - was at The Gold Dollar. It was a venue he would frequent often, not least because it was only a five-minute walk from his own studio. "You could have just forty or fifty people in there and it seemed like a good crowd. From that point of view, it was great for all these bands starting out."

The disparate nature of Detroit's community heart was conversely why The Gold Dollar held such appeal. "You didn't hang out in Detroit, but that's why we liked the Gold Dollar so much," opines Andy of Flying Bomb. "You really had to make an effort to go there. If you were bored, it wasn't just around the corner. It would be more specific than that, you'd be like, 'I have to see this band.' That's' the way it worked.

The first couple of times I went, I was really annoyed because the bands kept failing to show up. I drove in to see the Subsonics once and the band had got into town but then couldn't find The Gold Dollar. They drove around and around but were scared to get out of their car. It was a week night and the support was the Demolition Doll Rods, who played forever trying to stall. It was quite a drive from my house to The Gold Dollar, so afterwards I took to calling the venue to check it was okay."

From the point of view of The White Stripes and the numerous other bands that played at The Gold Dollar, the ethics of Neil Yee and his choice of acts was crucial, as Surge Joebot of Detroit veterans The Wildbunch (latterly Electric Six) explained to me: "For the Wildbunch, The Gold Dollar was HQ for a really long time. The guy that ran that place was real gutsy as far as booking anything. Most bands started out there. It was really, really neat, like having your friend's basement to party in. That venue was incredibly important. I don't know that any of this stuff would have happened otherwise."

The actual practicalities of the venue also made it a winner for the artists playing there, as Surge continues: "The stage was raised about a foot or so, which was fine, it was bigger than some places, we were quite happy to play there. I thought it was a pretty good sound system. I saw some great sounding shows there, and I could always hear all right onstage. They had a smoke machine. We used that a lot.

Plus the atmosphere behind the scenes - it was real casual between the bar tender, door people and the owner. For a good band it was an excuse to go pick up a few hundred bucks and get really, really tanked! Sometimes we would start so late that the bar would be forced to stay open well past close. It was funny, it would have made a really good sit-com. A lot of good personalities and funny stuff happening all the time."

Two of those personalities were Jack and Meg White. They were regulars at The Gold Dollar and therefore it was the only choice for the debut gig by The White Stripes. That first show came on 14 July 1997 - Bastille Day.

Neil Yee explains: "On Sundays we had an 'Open Mike Night' which was where we saw the first White Stripes show. I'd known Meg's older sister Heather for some time, after meeting her at some other show years before. She was one of the first people I'd met when I'd moved to Michigan. At this point, Meg had never done anything musically and I guess I'd seen Jack in a couple of bands but I didn't remember him from that. I just remember him because he was always around when I was hanging out with Meg and Heather and their family.

It was Mother's day and we were out with Meg and Heather's mum and Jack and a couple of other people. Jack said he was trying to put something together and wanted to try to record this new band on that first night. That was really the deal, he wanted me to record the band so that he could take a listen to it. On the actual night, there was hardly anyone there. You hear all these people saying they were there, but actually there were only a few open mike night regulars, ten people at most, I guess.

It was okay but not great. It was really basic, Jack has always been good, Meg was really terrible [Author's Note - she had only been playing two months]. She was playing simple beats but she wasn't really very consistent at all. She wasn't very accurate with her tempo, although to be fair in terms of hitting the drums she was relatively consistent. It's great to see that later developed a level of consistency but it sounded like a real struggle at the beginning. It was really an interesting thing to watch.

Because there wasn't much up there on stage it was pretty easy to engineer. And Jack was always right on the microphone so it wasn't really too difficult to engineer. In that size room with a band with three guitars you can get in trouble.

I think the payment for the recording of that first gig was actually that he re-upholstered a rocking chair for me. I didn't really know him too well. He just seemed like a really nice kid. You couldn't really have got this feeling that they were going anywhere. Nonetheless, Jack was really good, he seemed to be ambitious but you know he was just a kid. He didn't know what he was doing."

Ben Blackwell of Italy Records – Jack's cousin - was there along with a handful of others. "They played a handful of songs [Author's Note: one was 'Love Potion Number Nine']. I remember hearing a recording of that gig," he told me. "It was pretty rough, because Meg had never played on stage before. That gig wasn't formally booked or anything, they just showed up and played. Their first booked show was planned to be with Rocket 455 and 68 Comeback a while later, so the gig on Bastille Day was a good idea, Meg could get her bearings. There were a few missed beats or whatever but as a whole I thought it was cool."

Gary Graff, the aforementioned Detroit journalist has this to say about Meg's rudimentary drumming: "I think she would be the first one to acknowledge that she had to take all her cues from Jack. He had the vision, he knew how he wanted the drums, it was his sound and it matched what he was doing on guitar."

The first gig The White Stripes actually booked in advance was indeed a show with Rocket 455 and 68 Comeback, just a month after this first impromptu set on open mike night. Again, it was at The Gold Dollar.

At that show was Surge Joebot of the Wildbunch. "I'd seen Jack playing guitar in Two Star Tabernacle of course, a band I thought were really good. We went to see Rocket that night at The Gold Dollar and watching the White Stripes I remember thinking the guy had to have incredible balls to be singing like Geddy Lee. [Author's Note: Geddy Lee is the singer for Canadian rockers Rush. He has an uncomfortably high voice, an issue examined by Steve Malkmus in the lyrics of a Pavement song 'What about the voice of Geddy Lee? / How did it get so high? / I wonder if he speaks like an ordinary guy?']

Back then Jack was bringing furniture and backdrops and stuff from home, and dressing the stage up with the colours and whatnot. There was a vague air of performance art or something, which I've always felt was a big, unacknowledged aspect of Detroit rock. More so maybe than rock from other Midwestern cities. Bands from Chicago or Minneapolis or wherever can sometimes be real stern and stolid in their purveyance of cerebral rock or naturalist rock or whatever it is. Bands from Detroit are almost uniformly absurd in a way. Bands from here are extra-willing to make cartoons of themselves. Even a band like the Stripes, you know, there's a lot of emotional complexity to what their doing, but there's also this element of like, are these two for real? They look like a cartoon. And you can find that aspect in almost any Detroit rock band you care to name. All the good ones, anyway. And that's a tradition in this town, I think."

Back to that actual gig on the night, Surge continues: "Jack had his head shaved on the sides and there was like this red rooster hair on the top. There were other bass-less acts around such as Bantam Rooster so it didn't stand out in my mind as being that unusual a format. What I thought was unusual was Jack's approach. To my mind it was like something from Mars. Particularly in respect of the voice, the musical marriage, there was something real feminine about what they were doing but at the same time it was based on a lot of hard rock clichés. Actually her drumming is probably more macho than Jack's singing. It's that weird collision... everybody goes on about how it's just garage-type rock or blues-based, but I think there's all kinds of stuff going on with what they're doing. There's arena rock in there, folk, there are a lot of old early-twentieth century forms being used, vaudeville and show tunes. You see a lot of talk in the press about, 'Oh, it's a throwback or it's retro,' but in reality I think Jack's got a really wide range of influences going on, and he's synthesizing them in a really advanced, modern way. That night at the Gold Dollar it was just a weird thing to me.

I don't know if anyone's ever mentioned this, but I always thought a big unacknowledged influence in what they were doing was like this sort of wilful innocence, the whole child-like thing. Which was a big reaction against rocking and rockist impulses. But then, within that, they're all about rocking. It's really schizophrenic, but you don't see any seams. The next day somebody called me up and asked what I thought of that new band last night. I said, 'I thought they were really good, but they'll never catch on.'"

In the aftermath of the White Stripes latterday huge success, this first (booked) gig has become one that many people claim to have attended. 'If the number of people were there who have since claimed they were at that gig, they would have played the Pontiac Silver Dome," Gold Dollar owner Neil Yee states. He can obviously vouch for the sparsity of the actual crowd numbers. Dave Buick of Italy Records was indeed there and he maintains that there were more kids outside the venue when the band were playing than watching the show.

55

With this debut pair of shows under their belt, The White Stripes started to gig frequently and rehearse even more so. The following night they played in support of The Hentchmen. Johnny from that band recalls how Jack got this second gig: "We were walking down the street when Jack and Meg came by and said, "Hey! you're the Hentchmen!" They said we're starting up a band and that they would like to open up for us. Jack gave me his upholstery card - called Third Man Upholstery. About four months later I found the card and decided to call him up, because we needed an opener at The Gold Dollar. I called him out of the blue and so they did the show. We thought it was cool there was a new band in town. We didn't hear them at this point, they got the gig without us hearing a demo. I thought it was cool that he came up to us and approached us and based on that we had no idea what to expect. But we thought it was great. That first show we had we let them come over for the party afterwards. Jack came by with his little blue dog – it was a chow or something. He wasn't real social, I don't think. I never saw him around town before that. After that, we started doing gigs all the time with those guys. Maybe a dozen gigs we did that year with them. They were always professional and delivered a good show. We only went out of town with them once. We played in Cleveland with them and they were real fun to hang out with."

One 'solo' special gig Johnny Hentchmen remembers clearly: Jack played alone at the Garden Bowl room at The Magic Stick. "Jack went up alone with is guitar and we were all there. He did a lot of the songs that would appear on his first album. When I saw him do that I definitely knew that he belonged on TV! It was probably one of the best shows I've ever seen him produce."

The Gold Dollar was the favourite venue of choice, but The Magic Stick was also used a lot. Although many people I have spoken to insist there was no real momentum locally for quite some time, journalist Gary Graff saw many of the band's very early gigs and maintains that the Stripes did after all make an immediate impact: "The very idea of The White Stripes, it was such a curve ball, such an out-of-left-field concept. Guitar and drum only, a girl on drums. Also, they were so raw at first, the sound itself was so, *so* different from anything else we were hearing, even in the underground. There was rock going on, of course, but it was usually a four or five piece set-up, guitars, bass, drums, the normal rock 'n' roll band. Yet here was The White Stripes, just a guitar and drums and raw, unfinished really, almost joyfully so."

Surge Joebot disagrees and points out that the White Stripes being a duo was not as exceptional as some observers seem to make out. "There were other two piece around. Bantam Rooster was a pretty big band then, and the first people I knew who got to tour Europe. We were all like, *You're going where?!?* They were a two-piece, guitar and drums. An earlier version of the Wildbunch had just been the singer on guitar accompanied by a drummer. The bass-less approach had been popularised by Flat Duo Jets and Beat Happening, and a lot of bands were picking up on it as a way of shrugging off the sort of standard rock concerns. The Demolition Doll Rods were, in my mind back then, like *the* big band in Detroit. They were always touring the US and shit, and they were a bass-less trio. And there were other bands like Fez, who used all kinds of non-Rock instruments.

Now that I think about it, there was a lot of unorthodox shit going on, so that wasn't what made the White Stripes stand out, not in my mind. But their overall sound and look and the way they synthesized their influences struck me (and I think everyone) as nothing if not unique, right off the bat. But at the time, when they first started playing, their uniqueness didn't make them that unique, if that makes any sense. They were just another weirdo band in Detroit, one out of a hundred weirdo bands. Everybody was doing something different. It was a much less orthodox scene."

Many locals who saw this first batch of gigs commented that Jack's voice was too high and whiny, but overall the duo got off to a reasonable start. Maribel Restrepo of the Detroit Cobras noticed how, "All the girls used to call him the Great White Hope, because he was tall and handsome. They opened for everybody, including the Cobras. At first, you heard this Robert Plant screaming-woman thing. He's really got that honed now."

Jeff Meier of Rocket 455 was intrigued by Jack's live set-up. "Jack's equipment was basic stuff. He had a Silver Tone amp - it's just a catalogue item that kids buy when they are starting out to play guitar, it's big and it looks nice. He also had a reverb box that he plugged in to get that real narrower sound that he had. It's not the best piece of equipment you can buy, for sure, but it gets this sound that is unmistakable."

The White Stripes nascent days coincided with various other projects. Jack also played some shows with The Hentchmen briefly around this period (reportedly wearing a yellow suit) and went on to appear on their *Hentchforth* EP. Later in 2003, the track 'Hypnotize' from this period appeared on The White Stripes' fourth album, *Elephant*. The start of The White Stripes also fleetingly overlapped Jack's continuing work in Two Star Tabernacle. Ben Blackwell, later to work with his cousin Jack at Italy Records on The White Stripes early singles, recalls one show where Jack played in both bands: "The first time I saw The White Stripes was October 1997, down in Toledo. They opened for Two Star Tabernacle. The White Stripes were on first - Jack wore red and white for that set, then there was another band in-between them and then he came back out wearing something different for the Two Star show. But both sets were great. Two Star was a great band, they only did that one single but that wasn't that too good a representation of the way they sounded. I wish more people could hear more of that Two Star stuff because it was really, really rocking.

The White Stripes set was really, really primitive. There were probably about ten people there but it was one of the greatest gigs I'd ever seen. It was rough around the edges, but it was all really endearing. It didn't seem like ineptitude, just really, really wonderful."

CHAPTER 6

"Jimi said to me, 'The best thing you can do, brother, is turn it up as loud as it'll go.'"

Billy Gibbons of ZZ Top speaking in 1984 about advice given to him by Jimi Hendrix.

With The Gold Dollar becoming a thriving venue, the number of bands playing all the time and the quality of the music being made, the very first inklings of something special was starting to be felt in Detroit. The fuel for the fire was always – and still is – the live circuit. Ben Blackwell has an intriguing slant on why The Gold Dollar specifically, and the live scene in Detroit *per se*, was so crucial to the emergence of all these bands at this time. "People in Detroit seemed to be really slow to become technologically savvie, even simple stuff like getting a computer, logging on to the internet. So the vast majority would rely much more on personal interaction at clubs, bars and so forth. For example, people who went out on tour and had seen bands would come back and tell you to check out a certain act they had seen. So all their friends would check them out. Likewise with local acts. No one was reading a review on the web and watching a gig as a result of that web piece."

One aspect of the recent explosion of successful bands in Detroit that is hard to deny is the extent to which they help each other out and are so inter-linked. Everyone seemed to play occasionally for everyone else; they all have recorded, produced, mixed, cameo-ed on and helped out with each other's records; at many shows the small audiences are made up mostly of other bands… and so on. It is a refreshingly co-operative atmosphere and one that is unusual for many scenes.

Musicologists might point towards the city's poverty as a reason behind this laissez faire attitude. When faced with financial difficulties and a harsh life, people often gel together against the odds. There may be something in this, although no one is suggesting that the majority of Detroit bands suffered poverty similar to that which plagued the blues artists that many of this latest generation so revere. And yet Detroit is a firmly working class city, it is not a glamorous place, nor a particularly picturesque one and there is an underlying sense that the more dog-eat-dog mentality of more cosmopolitan cities would just seem so out of place there.

Yet, as with previous Detroit musical peaks, there was also a large influence from outside the confines of the city. One decidedly peculiar element of the Detroit music scene is that over the years and through various clusters of bands, much of the most exciting music has actually originated from areas outside of the city itself. The best example of this is Ann Arbor, a university town where the principal site of the University of Michigan is based, some forty five minutes drive west of Detroit. The city was home to many thriving industries, much of which was related to the University - contributions to the space programme and the training of actual astronauts were among the city's notable achievements. That said, University of Michigan itself was best known for studies in humanities and the arts, so in many ways it was a predictably fertile breeding ground for new bands and music. On March 9, 1945, the ribbon cutting ceremony was held for the newly completed multi-lane industrial highway from Michigan and Wyoming avenues in Detroit to the Willow Run bomber plant in Ann Arbor and thus the two communities became inextricably linked. Yet, despite such physical connections, the two areas have maintained distinct creative personalities.

Prior to the arrival of the Stooges, Ann Arbor witnessed what one conservative observer described in *The Pictorial History of Ann Arbor* as "mass frivolity" in the form of an anti-Vietnam demonstration consisting of "the nation's first 'teach-in'… utilizing films, discussion groups, and speakers, many sessions lasted all night in an effort to develop a coherent anti-war position. Later mass rallies and their support of 'trashing' or the digging of 'bomb craters' to rock music were sad declensions from the original." Clearly the city had a subversive beat to its heart.

As if to reinforce this theory, the Stooges made their debut there on Halloween night, 1967 and were based there for much of their career, spiritually as much as geographically. Back then, it was seen as a thriving artistic community and its attraction even pulled in Detroit city bands such as the Empty Fives, who were one of many acts to relocate to be nearer the hub of musical activity. While MC5 were still linked to Detroit itself – remember, their seminal album *Kick Out The Jams* was recorded live at Detroit's Grande Ballroom - Ann Arbor nevertheless remained central to the subversive and influential underground sounds coming out of this scene.

Moving into the late 1980s and 1990s, a similar creative community could be found in that area. Andy of Flying Bomb Records explained this to me: "In Detroit itself, at least until the arrival of The Gold Dollar, there really weren't many places to play for bands out there. There were just a few back entrance bars. Ann Arbor was actually boasted a much bigger scene. All the touring bands would go there. Some bands relocated there too, such as The Hentchmen. Other bands originated from Ann Arbor, like the Monarchs and the Paybacks were in Ann Arbor too. It seemed at times like everybody was in Ann Arbor."

Within the Ann Arbor community, there was a culture of house parties and it was at these gatherings more than formal gig venues, that many of the bands from the most recent incarnation of the Detroit music scene started and thrived. Despite its proximity to the University, very few of these acts were student bands.

Surge Joebot, latterly of Electric Six, was one of the musicians drawn to this area. "I grew up in Detroit but I left the city for a while after high school. It didn't seem like there was anything going on in Detroit, and we weren't savvy enough to know about it anyway. There was like some noisy rock, some alt country, but that was never really my interest anyway. So in 1994 I moved to Ann Arbor because I figured that was where the MC5 were from so therefore that must be a good place to start a band. And it turned out that everybody there was into Phish and blues stuff and all this like pop jam shit. But it didn't work out so we came back to Detroit in defeat and there was this huge scene going on!"

Despite this, Detroit could not boast such a lively and close-knit community spirit as Ann Arbor. "Detroit's not a really hang around town," muses Andy of Flying Bomb. "You don't really walk the streets of Detroit, see what's going on and go to record stores. That doesn't happen there. There's nobody around, on the streets. There'll be a mile of disused buildings and stuff like that then a store or maybe a club, but then more disused buildings and so on."

Likewise with the record labels in the area, the actual bands did not generally vie with each other for success or attention. "I always thought the whole thing in Detroit was very uncompetitive and I really liked that," says Surge Joebot. "You'll always find a small minority of assholes who view the scene as a competition. I always felt if you wanted it like that, then why didn't you go into sports instead of buying a guitar? Nevertheless, there were always a few who'd get upset when someone else has any degree of success, but especially in the early days there was none of that in Detroit. For example, when (Detroit band) Bantam Rooster got their first tour of Europe, it was a really exciting thing, because you think, 'Huh. So people are willing to invest in a band from Detroit and send them to Europe.' It was very heartening. Before that it felt like you were operating in a total vacuum, and then people started getting these tours.

Everybody sticks up for each other and everybody helps each other out. There are one or two exceptions, you know, but by and large … it may have something to do with the fact that the city's so small. I don't really know."

This burgeoning scene which The White Stripes thus found themselves part of was a conglomeration of all these elements, The Gold Dollar, the city's history, the Ann Arbor/Detroit factor to name but a few. Above all perhaps, was this all-pervading sense of community. "I think my favourite part of the whole story," says Andy of Flying Bomb, "was the mass of people who played together who in other cities would never have done so. You'd regularly get some all out crazy punk band that would knock all their equipment over at the end of their set, playing the same stage as some strange, introverted arty band. I guess everyone had their own tastes but no one seemed to object to anyone else's. Everyone was completely different from everybody else yet somehow it gelled. Maybe that was because there was no grand plan; also there was a sense that not belonging but being among all these other like-minded people that made you belong.

My feeling is that other scenes (that existed) around Detroit appeared to be more insular than that. For instance, the Techno scene was big already, but those Techno people stuck together and it was harder to break into those circles. Eminem and the Kid Rock scene was similar. Our scene was always 'anything goes'. It really didn't matter. If you had a band you could play and if it was good and people liked it, you got in."

Although the media has made much of the MC5/Stooges legacy and influence, Andy is at pains to disagree and point out the diversity of the musical environment that Jack White was surrounded by: "I'd be standing there in a gig and I'd hear two people talking and about Chuck Berry, Rhine Harry and the Pagans in one conversation. At the same time, the PA would be playing a Devo record and the next thing you know I'm having a conversation with someone about AC/DC."

Gary Graff has been a music journalist since 1977 and worked in Detroit since 1982, so is perfectly placed to offer a perspective on the reasons behind the explosion of music that came out of that city in the mid-to-late 1990s and beyond, taking The White Stripes with it. "Detroit has always been a creative place, dating way back to the southern migration of the twentieth century. You can trace many creative paths, such events gave birth to John Lee Hooker, and also gave birth to the Trad Scene which in turn led to the R&B of Jackie Wilson and Motown. A huge legacy."

62

Surge Joebot gives this insider's view of the musical melting pot from where The White Stripes spewed forth, particularly when faced with suggestions that the scene had a specific 'sound'. "No, not at all. At the time there was no one popular sound. There was a sense of sound factions around Detroit. You had your experimental bands, your rock bands, your pop bands, retro bands. Some stuff veered towards metal and some stuff like the Dirtys or the Clone Defects veered way into different kinds of punk and hardcore. And then, within each clique, every band usually had its own unique spin, too."

Of course, for specific bands involved in the scene at the time –such as The White Stripes – all this was theoretical hyperbole reserved for journalists and generally outsiders. These were just bands getting on with being bands. None more so than The White Stripes.

Every scene has a cluster of great bands, but also at least a coupe of excellent labels, record companies that somehow sum up the very essence of the bands they are releasing. Quite often these labels are little more than bedroom outfits, run by people ensconced within the ranks of the local underground, often fans who just want to put out records by bands they love. Sometimes these labels never amount to much of a commercial venture; other times, as with the global player that Sub Pop became, they can almost single-handedly alter the very fabric of the record industry.

What all of these labels have in common and at their very heart, is a deep and unblinking passion for the local music. Way back in Detroit in the 1980s, one ultra-underground example was Human Fly Records. Jeff Meier of Rocket 455 had some experience with this nascent label years before the White Stripes were even formed: "The owner was a big Gories fan and was real supportive of all his bands - when my band started he was a huge fan. I wouldn't say he was real organised but in his spare time he would do this label. I think he was just a big fan of music that was only just starting to happen. It didn't really make him any money I would presume. He just enjoyed doing it."

Another more established example of a Detroit label that existed in tandem with the scene that housed The White Stripes is Italy Records, set up by Dave Buick in the early 1990s. His first release was originally going to be a single by the Dirtys, motivated mostly by the fact that they hadn't got a record out and he felt they should have. He simply told them if they gave him a recording he would release it. They were quite slow getting something to him, and in the intervening months, Rocket 455 gave him a track and he put that out as Italy Records debut release.

Over the years, Buick's only assistance has been from the aforementioned Ben Blackwell, who takes up the tale: "The label was run out of Dave's house. He didn't have an office or anything. It was almost something for fun. He didn't do it full-time, he used to work in jobs in the day, usually in a record store or as a waiter.

The entire operation has always been very organic. For the most part he put out local bands. A good example of how he worked was a single he did by a band called the Cells, who were friends of the Hentchmen. He'd done a Hentchmen single and that band said, 'Why don't you check out the Cells?' - so he did a single with them. Gradually he started releasing out-of-town bands too but generally only those who played in Detroit a lot – the Greenhornes, the Soda Devils, and so on. At the time the Greenhornes recorded singles for Italy they were probably playing Detroit at least once a month."

Much later, Dave set up a web site in true Italy Records style. "A friend of his put up the site, it's still up. It's super rudimentary - there's no on-line ordering - Dave doesn't have an e-mail address. It is just really, really primitive, but it works."

Ben's own route to working with Italy was similarly relaxed: "Everyone just used to hang around in Detroit. I'm younger than a lot of other people (Author's Note: Ben was born in 1982). I knew Dave was doing Italy and I was just looking for something to do. Just being a bored kid or whatever. It ended up me talking to distributors for him and working on singles, The label never got to a huge operation but in terms of getting to know contacts, meeting people and learning how to run a record company and stuff like that, it was superb."

One of the bands that Dave Buick would release on Italy Records was The White Stripes. Ben recounts how the duo first came to work with Dave's label: "Dave had seen them at one of their earliest shows, round about 1997, and asked them to do a single. At the time, Jack didn't really know how things worked and thought they would have to pay Dave to do stuff. So Jack said 'No, no, we don't want to do it.' Dave saw him again some time later and again he said, 'Hey, listen we really want to do a single with you.' This time, Jack came out and said, 'Well, we don't want to pay for anything.' Dave said, 'You don't have to pay for anything! Just give me some songs and I'll put them out.'" This was late 1997.

In a back-to-basics style that would later become the quintessential calling card of The White Stripes, their debut single, 'Let's Shake Hands' was recorded in Jack's front room. "First off when The White Stripes said they were going to record 'Let's Shake Hands' as their debut single, I was confused," remembers Ben. "On the one hand, even if I listen to it now, I still think that Jack's guitar solo is up there with 'A Whole Lotta Love'. I'd never heard anything like that. It's incredible, it's like where the hell did that come from?

Yet at the same time, I thought they had many better songs than that at the time, 'Jimmy The Exploder' and 'Screwdriver' being just two examples. I said, 'Why are you going to do that track?' and they said, 'Well, if we were to do an album, we'd want to save those other songs for that.' It definitely wasn't their best song and what confused me was, this is the first time *anyone's* going to hear you, so why don't you give it your best song? But they were thinking ahead, even then."

Despite having apparently no knowledge of the business machinations of the music industry whatsoever, Jack certainly had, by contrast, a very focussed vision of what his band were aiming for. "He was definitely confident and sure of the music and how he wanted it to sound," noticed Ben. "He asked Dave if they could do the single in two colour vinyl. He wanted it in white and red. Dave had never done coloured vinyl before but he said, 'Yeah, sure'. He wanted the actual label colours changed too, to be red and white instead of the usual black and pink. Jack also wanted a little insert, a little quote from George Washington and Dave said 'Sure' to all that too. This was a bunch of things which Dave had never done before but he was into it. At the time, you'd think it would be cool to sell one hundred copies and have another 1000 sitting in your attic."

The quote Jack used from Washington was this: "We take the stars from the blue union from heaven, the red from our mother country, separating it by white stripes, thus showing we have separated from her, and the white stripes shall go down to posterity representing liberty."

"I was looking for a quote to put in our first single that would sum up the band," said Jack later, "and I swear to God I opened an encyclopaedia at the thrift store and I opened up to the page with that quote in it. I couldn't believe it."

However, Ben is quick to extinguish any suggestion that Jack was being an awkward rock star: "It was much more like friends chatting. Like 'Hey, can you do this?' Jack wasn't demanding about anything. It was just messing around, he didn't think anything of it, it was no big deal. Jack and Meg were just sweethearts to work with in the office."

So what did The White Stripes very first venture on to vinyl sound like? Exactly like you would want The White Stripes debut recording to sound! It is visceral, distorted, abrasive and utterly fabulous. The drums are basic, the guitars violently shredding and the overall effect unsettling but at the same time compelling. It was backed with 'Look Me Over Closely' written by Terry Gilkyson and Mitch Miller and originally recorded by Marlene Dietrich in 1953.

Within the small circles of the Detroit scene, The White Stripes debut singles did make a few (albeit small) waves. "In town," recalls Ben, "no one in Detroit was surprised about it because people had known about the band already. It was like, 'Oh yeah, The White Stripes are cool.' I think it fitted in with that whole garage scene, you know. Yet at the same time it had some discerning marks that made it a little different."

At the same time, they were hardly big news - Dave Buick was repeatedly annoyed/amused by the constant misspelling of their name, with variations such as White Strike, the Light Strikes or The White Stripe. At one Toledo show, they were billed as The White Lines.

Although 'Let's Shake Hands' was well received on a very small local scale, at least in the opinion-forming bars and clubs around Detroit, Ben is very blunt and honest about the actual commercial success of the debut release: "The single's impact? The immediate impact was that there was no immediate impact. I think The White Stripes, the first time they had the record on sale they shifted three copies, And one of those guys bought it because they thought it was someone out of Black Sabbath!"

Other than at gigs, local stores would stock the debut single. Buick had always done mail order from his house and he had also started dealing with smaller independent local distributors who would take maybe ten copies. Not many perhaps, but to be fair, this was The White Stripes very first release.

There were sporadic albeit low profile reviews of the single. A magazine in the mid-West called *Noises From The Garage* said, "'Let's Shake Hands' sounded like the Oblivions…" Ben Blackwell picks up the tale: "One far more crucial little development came when the record was placed in the Asterisk catalogue - Asterisk being a label out of Bellingham, Washington. They wrote in the description that "The White Stripes are the best thing in Detroit since The Gories." They might have had a question mark after that, like "the best thing in Detroit since the Gories?" But we all freaked out nonetheless, 'Oh my God, it's so cool!

That quote worked for The White Stripes for some time to come. Later that year, Mudhoney came to town, so me and Dave went to the show together. Dave took them some singles and Steve Turner looked at The White Stripes vinyl and said, 'I hear these guys are better than The Gories!'

We were stunned, we just said, 'Oh my God, it's so cool that Steve Turner knows The White Stripes.' We were all excited about any little word of mouth."

Nonetheless, the 1000 copies (not 500 as has been reported) pressed of 'Let's Shake Hands' did not sell out at that point. Indeed, it wasn't until mid-2001, just prior to the release of *White Blood Cells* that those initial copies finally ran out. Italy Records did a reprint of 2000 copies and still has some stock left at the time of writing. Jack and Dave still keep in touch to this day and the band often contact him if they need copies of these singles for special sales on tour.

Following on quite swiftly from 'Let's Shake Hands', came The White Stripes' second single, 'Lafayette Blues', also recorded in Jack's house and also for Italy Records. The single was a blast, a maelstrom of shattering power chords, countless time changes and booming drum beats. Jack's oft-distorted vocals are at their most obtuse, barely discernible from the noise backing him but essential nonetheless. Some observers referenced Led Zeppelin but this comparison seems a little forced. Flip the single over and you have the polar opposite, an acoustic ballad called 'Sugar Never Tasted So Good' which is almost obviously stating the band's breath of vision (later seen on the debut album too).

Jack and Meg were always at the very centre of any design decisions: "How much did they input? It was all them," explains Ben. "The first edition folds out with a bunch of pictures and a little strip of paper that had all the French street names in Detroit. It was viewed more like an art project than a record.

In really early copies, Jack inserted French franc WWII occupation notes in there too. There's a certain number with F10 notes, a certain number had F5 notes and one had a F50 note. There was also a quote from Marquis de Chastellux plus a photocopied picture of the Marquis de Lafayette shaking hands with George Washington. At the time we thought that was really interesting because the first single had a quote from George Washington in it, and was called 'Let's Shake Hands'; since then Jack had found a picture of these two shaking hands. I think the associations got even weirder too - Lafayette ended up giving George Washington the keys to the Bastille and the White Stripes first show had been on Bastille Day - it is almost cosmic, a predetermined thing."

Patti, wife and partner of Andy from Flying Bomb, designed the cover for the White Stripes second single for no charge. "We did most of them for free," recalls Andy, "just because he was a friend of ours. And he also gave us a lot of freedom. Patti does a lot more of the design work than I do - she says I take care of a lot of the talking! They weren't happy with their first EP cover, how it looked, so we did the second one and then later we actually re-designed the debut single cover too."

In true Spinal Tap style, once out of Andy's capable hands, the record sleeves for 'Lafayette Blues' arrived late for the October 1998 show at which Jack and Meg had planned to sell their second single for the very first time. Keen to launch the record regardless but anxious to avoid embarrassment, Jack and Dave Buick promptly sat down at the back of the venue after the sound check and painstakingly hand-painted fifteen copies of the sleeve, then numbered them individually. They did fifteen to make extra sure there were enough.

These now-highly collectible singles cost just $6 at that show. More intriguingly, as each sleeve was done by hand (they each did about half), every single one is unique. Ben bought a copy for himself, even though he worked with Italy Records! "At the time I remember thinking 'Oh my God, we're asking six bucks - there's no way these people are going to buy them.' It's like some inner sanctum or a secret club now, anyone who has one of these knows everyone else who has one! We ended up with $90 in merchandise cash just from those singles and I remember thinking that that was so much money.

One owner put his copy on e-Bay for $999 but eventually sold it for $750 to a fan in the Netherlands. That is a lot of money, but think about it this way. If The White Stripes continue to succeed in the way that they have so far… imagine how interesting it would be to have a hand-painted single from Mick Jagger, that's how I would consider it."

This rare batch of hand-designed singles shared its individuality with the bulk pressing of 1000 copies. "The pressing plant had failed to clean out the vats before they pressed the record," explains Ben. "It was supposed to be on white vinyl. When they told us they had forgotten to clean out the vat, we said, 'Oh ok, so what was the other colour in there?'… 'Red!'

Remarkably, the effect of the red remnants and the main white colour was a kinda like peachy swirl. Some copies were totally pink - probably about five to ten really early copies, but as the pressing went on and on it changed into a pink and white swirl and then eventually just a white vinyl with almost a pink marble in it. The earlier your record is the pinker it is! That was totally just a mistake… just destined to happen."

As with the debut single, the initial pressing of 1000 copies (again not 500) lasted until the summer of 2001, then a re-pressing of another 1000 copies also sold out much quicker around the time of the band's third album.

Inevitably, with the subsequent global success of The White Stripes, much more of a spotlight has been placed on labels such as Italy Records. Yet, still many of their early releases remain modest sellers, as Ben points out: "The original single by the Dirtys was done in the edition of 1,000. Dave has maybe a box of those left, so it's probably sold about 950 copies. That took about four years. The Rocket 455 single, he's probably got 200 left of those. Some of his singles have sold out, some are still available." There is something refreshing about the fact that Italy have not 'remixed and remastered' every recording they have in their archive that even vaguely relates to Detroit and/or the White Stripes. Some indie labels, it seems, can remain true to their roots and all credit is due to them for that.

Prior to the White Stripes' eponymous debut album (and in between first and second singles) they recorded a track for a Christmas sampler record released by Flying Bomb Records. "The first time I saw them," recalls label boss Andy, "they were playing The Gold Dollar opening for the 68 Comebacks. There were not many people there and actually the White Stripes were not a strong band back then. They were entertaining but they weren't that strong. They played songs like 'St James Infirmary Blues' and even some covers. Later, Jeff Meier from Rocket 455 and the Cobras introduced me to Jack. He was just a quiet kid and we started talking.

As with Italy Records, Flying Bomb Records was equally born out of a love of local bands, two people just wanting to play a part in releasing cool music. Head of Flying Bomb, Andy takes up the tale: "It was essentially set up due to what we saw as a necessity for a label. There were two bands, Chinese Millionaires and Dancing Rooster, who were both really good. Originally, we had shopped those bands around the labels we knew and but no one seemed really interested, so around late 1995 we decided to start Flying Bomb and do it ourselves. We basically put out stuff that nobody else seemed interested in putting out. If somebody else was interested in putting stuff out then we didn't bother!

Detroit was hardly awash with labels, big or small. There was Motown of course, but for garage band such as The White Stripes, the potential to get a record released locally was pretty slim. "There really were no labels in Detroit to speak of," aggresses Andy. "Right around the same time we started, Dave Buick started Italy Records. The great thing about it was that there was no competition, they would say, 'Oh, I'm putting this out,' and we would be like, 'Oh good, we don't have to now!' That was the mentality, we never fought over bands, Dave and I. We even sold his stuff in our catalogue. Things were just like that back then.

For our Christmas 1997 sampler, we said to The White Stripes 'give us a song for it' and Jack went 'Oh no, I don't know what to write for a Christmas song.' I said, 'But it's red and white, it should be right up your alley,' and he went, 'Oh yes!'

We were pleased because we wanted diversity on the record and it was a killer song that he put forward, a real cute children's song. Jack recorded the track in his living room, he borrowed an eight-track recorder and then took it over to local producer Jim Diamond who mixed it with him. We eventually took all the songs for the compilation to Jim Diamond's to complete the record.

We pressed five hundred copies only, because most of the bands were totally unknown. Years went by and the record didn't sell out at all, it was in the catalogue for ever. Then one day we discovered copies were being sold on e-Bay for $100 and we had it in our catalogue for $4! So we took them out of the catalogue and throw them on e-Bay!

By now, The White Stripes were beginning to gather some decent momentum. Neil Yee of The Gold Dollar was still surprised that Meg was making such a go of the band. "Meg is the last person you'd ever think of becoming a rock star. Very reserved, like her sister. She'd never done anything with music before. She'd hung out with musicians and that was about it. As far as I know she'd never played any instrument. To be honest, she didn't seem to have any natural ability. It was really odd. Heather thought it was really odd when Meg quit her job and said all she was doing was the band, we were like, 'that's really weird'."

CHAPTER 7

"I don't have the blues so I don't play the blues. I'm a pretty happy guy."

Jack White was still not exclusively playing with The White Stripes. Having left Two Star Tabernacle, Jack had joined a highly thought of local band called The Go. Jack was playing in the Go as late as 1999, when The White Stripes were also simultaneously gigging around Detroit. Oddly enough, some of the Go gigs were at a now-defunct techno club and therefore one of the very few occasions when the rockers in Detroit blended to some degree with the techno heads who also populated the city.

Bobby Harlow of the Go saw Jack initially while he was playing for Two Star Tabernacle. He later told Brian McCollum how they came to approach him. "Jack was laying back playing great guitar, singing harmonies with Dan Miller. He just had a great stage presence - he looked really cool, he looked comfortable. He wasn't a phoney at all. I said to John (Krautner of The Go), 'Let's go up front and look at this guy.' Dave Buick (of Italy Records) had already put out a White Stripes single at that point. Later, Jack was over at Dave's house, so John and I went over there. 'Hey, Jack, we've got a question for you,' and Jack said, 'Yes, already, absolutely wanna join, count me in.' We said, 'All right!'

Whenever we practiced at Jack's house upstairs in his room. For the record: Jack's house is red and white. The whole damned thing is red and white. The attic - the practice room - has got an American flag, all done in red and white. He's full-blown!"

It is clear that for a while, Jack did not see The Go as just another practice session. Andy of Flying Bomb has this to say: "He got a little more interested in The Go for a while. They were pretty popular. He also did some recording with the Hentchmen and with the Soledad Brothers. He was actually quite smart, he liked to work with lots of people and learn the tricks of the trade. When we worked with Jack, he said, 'I'm recording myself and you've got to pay for Jim Diamond, he knows how to mix and knows what we like and I'm not taking any chances.' It was a good, considered approach. Working in so many bands and with so many people like that was really good for him."

The Go began to gather a momentum which was reinforced by their superb debut album, which it is fair to say made them the foremost band in the Detroit area at that time – some would say they remain the most important Detroit band after the Gories. Matt Smith of Outrageous Cherry produced this album and tells the tale of Jack's involvement. "When I saw the Go live for the first time, of all of the bands I'd seen in Detroit I thought I'd finally seen one that was as good as the Rolling Stones. People were telling me, "Oh, they can't even tune their guitars, they can't write songs!" but I thought that they were something spectacular. The Go gave me a four track demo that I listened to and thought was absolutely the best I'd heard out of Detroit outside the Stooges and MC5. So I went up to them and told them "you should get in touch with my friend (producer of the Modern Lovers and Verse Two) Kim Foley, maybe he can make a record with you guys and actually sell it to a record company or something.

I called Kim up and told him. I said, 'I saw this band play and there were like these biker chicks talking to each other saying, these guys look exactly like the fucking Easy Beats, and he's like "oh, the Easy Beats are like my favourite group of all time.' So Kim tried to intervene in various places on their behalf. Then they asked him to produce them - Kim couldn't, so then the Go asked me to do it.

Right before we got to work on the record, Jack joined the group and that coincided with us getting signed to Sub Pop. The early Go gigs – they were just a four piece – like all the great bands in Detroit, their first gigs were totally shambolic and they didn't have their shit together at all. But I recognised the substance of it through the chaos and I think that's true of all the great bands from Detroit.

Once Jack had joined, it took a couple of gigs for the chemistry to click. But by the time we made the record they were absolutely mind-blowing so I just went to the studio and recorded the album in a week. It was a pretty quick affair.

With Jack in the five-piece, it was a pretty magical chemistry. It was really pretty astounding. Yet, before we went in the studio, Jack was pretty suspicious of my involvement. I didn't know him so well and so we had to have a lot of meetings before we actually set to work on the record. We would meet at the Clock Restaurant where we just basically sat drinking coffee and I had to reassure Jack that he'd be available to do whatever overdubs he needed to do. He just seemed really uneasy or suspicious about the thing. And then eventually he chilled out and we got down to making the record and everything went fine.

The album was done at Jim Diamond's (Ghetto Recorders studio, see below). Matt was mightily impressed with Jack's guitar work: "I think he's a great guitar player. He reminds me of an old Detroit band called the Third Power. His guitar playing is a real visceral sort of sound. He definitely puts his soul - mental and physical - into every solo which is what was really necessary for the Go."

Jack was also very exacting about his own parts. "There were little things that happened like we recorded the album really quickly and the whole time I'd be asking everyone in the band, 'what do you think? Does this sound alright? Is this cool?' Sometimes we'd do a few takes of the song, but generally nearly everything on the album was a first take. A few of the tracks are actually demos we recorded in Jack's living room – it's not really listed or noted properly on the record – but some of those tracks we just recorded on broken microphones in Jack's living room and then I took them and mixed them as rough mixes. I mixed five songs in thirty minutes. Three of those ended up on the album.

But the thing was, after we finished the record we were getting ready to mix and had gotten nearly everything recorded and everybody seemed basically very happy. Jim comes running into the control room and says, "Matt – Jack thinks he's going to re-do all his solos," and I'm like, "no, we're done. I'm mixing." I went in there and said, "Jack you didn't think you were going to re-do all your solos right now did you?" and he's like "Well, I wanted to just go through the tapes and just listen to all my parts and re-do some things." The thing was we made a CD of the instrumental versions at the beginning of the sessions so everyone could listen to them at home and ascertain if there was anything that needed to be changed."

In the end I said, "Look, we're about to start mixing. You go home and listen to the CD and if you hear any solos that you're not happy with, just come back tomorrow morning and we'll fix it all before I finish the rest of the mixes." So he just walked out of the room and started slamming doors and then left the studio without saying "bye" to anybody. So, what that means I don't know. Whatever his complaints were about it I couldn't even guess. To me it's a classic record. I think we ended up fixing one guitar solo."

Matt was relieved: "The thing about the Go was that these guys were totally fucking weird – if you didn't get them in one take, next take they'd slow the tempo down halfway. I mean, a song that sounded like MC5 one minute, then five minutes later sounded like the Grateful Dead! Five minutes later it sounded like Randy Newman. With the Go it wasn't even a question of spontaneity, it was a question of capturing it on tape before these guys personalities morphed into something completely different."

Halfway through the record some kind of weird tension started to emerge, between Jack and the group. I think he entered the Go hoping to have a little more control over the whole thing perhaps, I'm not sure.

I have some demos somewhere where he had worked on some of his songs with them. He co-wrote some of the songs on the album, but by the end of the record there was this tension. I mean we'd made this great record but I didn't know what was going on.

The record was sounding fantastic but by the end of it he came up to me in the studio one day and was like, "We've got to talk," and I'm like, "Alright, it's forty bucks an hour – let's talk!" and he's like "the synthesiser's go to go" and I'm like "well, have a meeting with your band about it, discuss it. I think the synthesiser sounds nice." You know what I mean? It sort of turned into one of those situations. Then the record was finally done, the band I guess they were just finding it difficult to communicate with Jack and he ended up not being in the group anymore."

This seemed very unfortunate because the Go were tipped by many as the band most likely to make it from this current cluster of Detroit bands. "When the album, *Whatcha Doin',* came out," continues Matt Smith, "some people said the record changed their lives like the first of the two Stooges records. They were saying it was the greatest rock 'n' roll record they'd ever heard and that it restored their faith in rock 'n' roll. I certainly feel that way. I feel that we'd done something that was definitely a template for the future of rock 'n' roll. I think we all felt that way. Including Jack.

Yet, conversely, some reviewers tore it, accusing the Go of being really decadent and horrible. There is this underlying sexual under current for sure but I think people hadn't heard that in music for twenty years, that was all part of it."

Jack parted company with the band before the album was released. Pretty soon after the Go went out on the road to promote the record. Matt Smith continued, "He just concentrated his energy on The White Stripes.

Even though he and Meg began to have relationship problems, somehow he managed to keep it all going, which is pretty impressive to me because every other Detroit band is always spending half their life dealing with personnel changes, people flipping out."

Some people wondered if Jack had backed the wrong horse. "The Go were basically touring and selling out shows all over the country. It was taking on all the appearance of a phenomenon. Then we did the second Go album with a different guitar player – Jack was replaced by Dion Fisher – which all of us thought was ten steps further forward from the first record. Sub Pop heard it and there was a little conflict and ultimately the record was not released, the Go were dropped from Sub Pop and they basically became inactive. It's still not clear exactly what happened but basically their whole momentum just got stifled."

Matt Smith thinks that the Go remain a classic band despite this earlier misfortune: "I've seen a lot of bands in Detroit, a lot of great bands and I still feel that they were and are the best of the lot. Period."

In retrospect, it wasn't just the age-old 'musical differences' that led to Jack's departure; the Sub Pop deal might have tied any of Jack's other future work - including that of The White Stripes who were already in existence - to that label. This was not something Jack was comfortable with.

Matt has much admiration for Jack's work since: "Jack just went and did exactly what the Go's original plan was – he released three albums in two years. And he didn't stop touring, he didn't sit around arguing about mixes and he didn't argue about personnel changes – he just went out and toured and worked his ass off."

Despite their past differences, Bobby Harlow of the Go told Brian McCollum how he is undimmed about his opinion of Jack: "He's one of the most talented guitar players I've ever met, and I have nothing but respect for him. To have a focused vision like Jack does, there's no way he can compromise that, where somebody can step in and say, "I think you oughta play like this, Jack." It would be an insult, really."

Later, Jack would reminisce about his live shows with t he Go as an easy ride compared to the demands of The White Stripes: "I enjoyed that so much because all I did was play the guitar. I didn't have to do anything."

CHƎPTER 8

"There's a fine line between fishing and standing on the river looking like an idiot."

Anon.

Every key protagonist I have spoken to about the key factors in The White Stripes/Detroit story is keen to acknowledge two very simple practical elements which were essential to the very lifeblood of this recent upsurge in music in that city: the aforementioned Gold Dollar music venue and the Detroit studios of producer Jim Diamond. His work with Jack and Meg would prove absolutely pivotal in the evolution of The White Stripes.

Jim Diamond's production credits and band associations read like a Who's Who of recent Detroit music. Apart from his own band, Jim Diamond's Pop Monsoon, he also plays/has played in The Dirtbombs, the Couvairs and the Witches. His production credits are even more extensive, with engineering nods on early Dirtbombs records and the first long player by the Von Bondies too as well as work with solo star Troy Gregory; he recorded the song 'Danger! High Voltage' for The Wildbunch which would later prove to be a breakthrough single for that band under the new moniker of Electric Six (Surge Joebot, formerly of that band told the author Jack was *not* singing backing vocals on this track, as widely reported) – Jim also played sax on this track and later provided some vocals and guitar for their 'Gay Bar' hit single; production of all three Bantam Rooster albums and countless singles by that band (he plays himself on several tracks); recorded the first and last album by the Dirtys; as well as recording and remixing work on releases by the Blowtops, the Screws, the Baseball Furies, the Jon Spencer Blues Explosion, Andre Williams, the Come Ons to name but a small selection. According to Matt Smith of Outrageous Cherry, "Jim was really the first person from outside of Detroit, who started to notice that there was something going on here."

Jim Diamond grew up some twenty miles south of Detroit city. By his early teens had already become fascinated by music. Like millions of others in his peer group, it was an obsession that never left him: "I've been playing music since I was thirteen, hanging out in rock bands and so on. Eventually I went to college and then on to University where I learnt

76

a little bit about audio and video production. While other people listen to what the musicians are doing, I started to pick out the production, trying to see how things had been done, learn about other people's production techniques. Similarly, I tended to idolise producers, mainly British names such as Micky Most and George Martin. All those kind of people I really admire. As far as what I do now with production and studio work, most of it is self-taught. I lived in Arken, Texas for about three years which was a good experience musically. After that I came back up to Michigan, although I didn't actually live in Detroit proper until about 1995."

Once ensconced in Detroit, Jim spent his first two years freelancing at small local studios, recording "horrible bands" but at the same time immersing himself in the new music that was beginning to bubble under. The freelance job was initially not providing sufficient income on its own, so Jim also worked in a steel fabrication factory to supplement his production wages. For many years, however, he had aspired to running his own studio so this testing situation was only ever going to be a stop-gap.

"I finally started getting a few pieces of equipment together, here and there, and then together with a friend of mine, I found a big loft downtown with lots of space. You hear a lot of stories about multi-million dollar studios - this loft was a former poultry processing factory. The room immediately had a great ambience and a great sound so I never did a thing to it. I walked in and didn't spend a penny on it." Jim fittingly christened the studio Ghetto Recorders.

With so much emphasis being placed on Jack's choice of antiquated studio equipment (and so much mythology about its exact age - see later), it might be easy to think that the name Ghetto Recorders was chosen because of its modest selection of older gear. Not so, this was a mere economic - "A lot of my equipment here is of the older variety," explains Jim, "but that is just because it's what I could afford. And I found out later that it really does sound great too. But there's digital tools I use too. Yes, I've made some great sounding records on an eight-track and a little twelve channel mixing board from the mid-1980's, but I don't think that's the most important part of the process."

At this juncture, the Detroit scene was still very much small-scale and local, not even national, so Jim was offering a service for a distinctly limited (and usually penniless) market. "I'd only recorded a few bands, but they were mostly bands that I didn't like. It was finally when I got into my own studio that I was able to start doing things that I just liked to hear and wanted to really produce. I didn't just want to be an engineer.

I convinced Tom Potter, the singer with Bantam Rooster (also of the Dirtbombs) to record in my new studio. I said, 'I've got an eight-track, I'm trying to make a stab at a studio by myself down here. I'd really love to offer you a record for next to nothing. It started from there."

That first double Bantam Rooster record was a pivotal one for me. They had been to Europe which was pretty rare for a band from this area at the time. They were getting some indie credibility and, of course, they were a two-piece band, one of a few similar duos at the time.

Mick Collins and I started to do a little work together that year as well. It just started happening all at once in the summer of 1997/98. Before I knew it, I had Andre Williams one week and Kim Folly in for the next week. So that was great experience for me. Over time, I met all these different kinds of people, the work started coming in more and more and it seemed like there were a lot of similarities between these individuals I was working with. That said, it was most definitely not a scene as such. No one set out to make a scene. We just found ourselves mixing with a lot of like-minded individuals, in terms of their music, their approach and their ethics. I can't single out exactly why, but it just seemed to be happening all at once."

Jim's production reputation quietly gathered momentum quickly and within a matter of months he was the first choice of any self-respecting local band, including The White Stripes.

Sympathy For The Record Industry was a leading, albeit small independent label based in California, to whom The White Stripes relocated for their third single. This first record with the new label - released as clear seven inch vinyl only - was the grinding track, 'The Big Three Killed My Baby', which Jack had valiantly but ultimately in vain tried to persuade Andre Williams to record. Lyrically it seems to hint at some vague commentary on the redundant Detroit car industry, the most political the White Stripes would come for some time, but this was really little more than a vibrant, thrilling guitar blast (again it resurfaced on the debut album). It was backed with 'Red Bowling Ball Ruth' which only ever appeared on this release, possibly because unlike many classic Stripes tracks, the melody is weak and the guitar sound a tad formulaic.

All this was but a teaser for the forthcoming debut album, also on Sympathy and released in mid-June, 1999. Jeff Meier was to play a central part in The White Stripes being offered the chance to record their first album: "Right after Italy put out 'Let's Shake Hands', Dave Buick gave me some copies. Geoff Evans from Memphis was playing in town and staying at my house - he's a big music fan as well. After the gig, we were back at my place listening to records, just having a good time and I put on 'Let's Shake Hands' and said, 'Check this out, they've just recorded this you know.' He flipped his lid, he went mad. I gave him a couple of copies and he immediately passed it on to Long Gone John (who ran Sympathy For The Record Industry). Soon after, Geoff called me and said Long Gone really liked the record and could he have Jack's number. I don't like giving out people's phone numbers so I phoned Jack and I said, 'This guy wants to put out your records - can I give him your number?' and Jack was like, 'Hell, yes!'"

Ben Blackwell explains why he and Dave Buick were not surprised when The White Stripes went to another label for the debut album. "Long Gone John at Sympathy had just put out the Detroit Cobras first record. At that stage in a band's career, when someone is offering to pay for a full-length, it is very tempting of course. Plus, for Italy Records it was not really financially viable to pay for an entire album. The only long-playing, non-45 that Italy ever did was a mini LP by the Hentchmen. We did 1000 copies of that and Dave still has some left."

So the debut album was scheduled to be recorded and the studio of choice was Jim Diamond's Ghetto Recorders. Part of The White Stripes peculiar mentality was to set parameters for each album. These would change as they became more successful, but for this very first record they wanted to keep the experience as fast, DIY and ultimately as cheap as possible.

Jim Diamond vividly recalls the degree of Jack's focus: "He was pretty careful about the studio work, in my experience with him. Back then, none of these bands had really made many records before. But Jack was always responsible, professional, turned up on time and so forth. We had a good time.

All of the recording was done on a two-inch, sixteen-track machine. Jack's got a real good idea of what he wants to hear. That was always my impression of working with him. A lot of it was rehearsed, you could tell they practised. Of course, way back then Meg was just very basic on the drums, she wasn't a John Bonham or anything like that. She was literally just starting out on her instrument.

Subsequently, we had to do a lot of takes, sometimes multiple takes - but it was never a problem. With Jack it was different. He'd played longer, in Two Star Tabernacle and all those other bands."

The obsession with simplicity is a trait that has been central to The White Stripes appeal and image, but it is clear from Jim Diamond's

79

experience that this is no media creation, no forced abstinence: "I had Megan in one corner of the room where I set up an amp and a mike because I wanted a big drum sound. We had some ideas and tried out a few different microphones. For the vocals, Jack actually played through an old guitar amplifier, so it purposefully sounded dirty. Dirtier than it really was. Everyone does it now, they try to make it sound nastier than it really is. But this was a very direct way of recording."

Much has been made of Nirvana's debut album, *Bleach*, being recorded for a few thousands dollars. With *The White Stripes* the story is similar, although of course the sales of each respective record are currently vastly different. Jim continues: "You have to understand this record was made for $2000. I remember when I said, 'Here's your studio bill,' Jack said to me, 'Oh my God, this is the biggest cheque I have ever written.' I said, 'Well, most other records that come out of here we usually make for under $5000.' People don't understand that. They don't think that's possible. The White Stripes record was $2000 and it would have been even less had we not spent a lot of time tracking and doing multiple takes of different songs."

Remarkably, given this fact, the whole first album was still completed in lightning fast time. "It was probably five, six days maybe a week in total," recalls Jim. Even that wasn't five days in a row." This brevity is part of the appeal: "I think that the records that I do generally and that Jack's done with me speak for themselves. I think they sound pretty real and organic, rather than overly polished, where producers and bands have just sucked the life out of things. Nonetheless, with the sort of budgets The White Stripes were on, and even though Jack was obviously very focussed, usually those kind of records would just disappear and the bands weren't heard from too much after that."

There's a fundamental problem in trying to represent blues music in the twenty-first century. We are so far away from the origins of what blues music is and was, and the format has been used and abused over so many decades, that it remains almost impossible to treat any 'new' music *just* as blues.

The blues as a musical form dates back well into the nineteenth century and probably long before that. Repeated phrasing, insistent rhythms, subject matter based upon the daily ups and downs of the ordinary man and woman's experience, trace back well into the pre-colonial days of African folk music. Brought to the new world under the slave migrations of the eighteenth and nineteenth centuries, African musicians carried with them their own indigenous folk music and retained and developed its traditions in their new environments. Blues, with its familiar twelve-bar format, grew out of this tradition as musicians who could liven up a party or entertain a group of poor and disenfranchised people became valuable and respected members of their society. Illicit drinking parlours and juke joints often had a piano to hand – in a sense, it is likely that the piano was the first truly American blues instrument. The guitar, meanwhile, while mimicking in its box/neck/string construction many traditional African instruments, also allowed musicians to become travelling entertainers, moving from one joint to another and from town to town as work allowed.

Early recordings show that - while the familiar and traditional blues of guitar players such as Robert Johnson were popular - so these same musicians played boisterous, happy piano rags, pop songs of the day, dance music and music hall songs. Blues players were entertainers within the early African American community, as likely to make you party as to declaim the loneliness and loss inherent in the classic blues song. The blues did not have to be sad and sombre - you could have a ball and dance as well.

With the urban development in the United States between and during the two world wars of the twentieth century, many African Americans migrated from the rural states to the cities, and with that came an urbanisation of the blues from its original country roots. Often within two generations, a family might have left Africa, settled in rural America, and been uprooted and divided again as its members moved to the conurbations. Electrification, and the development of amplified guitars in the thirties, meant that - just as jazz and dance bands could play before bigger and bigger audiences - a single electric blues player could entertain ten times as many people as only a few years previously, and the increasingly sprawling ghettos of the American industrial cities provided just such an audience. Out of this development came the wonderful, roughly-amplified guitar sounds of Memphis, Chicago and elsewhere.

Some of the most evocative music of the twentieth century was born in these centres, with fabulously-named players moving around and out of the Mississippi delta states and freely from city to city. The blues format influenced the developing jazz scene, gave birth to edgy, band-formatted rhythm and blues and, mixed with a little bit of country shuffle, rock 'n' roll. Through the post-war years and into the 1950s and 1960s, a generation of future rockers - fuelled by Elvis and Little Richard - found a darker, more urgent inspiration in the founding fathers of the blues. The blues renaissance in London in the 1960s brought many artists back into the public eye of what was now a global entertainment industry rather than the bars and whorehouses of Memphis and Louisiana.

This is where the blues began to lose its focus. While British bands such as John Mayall's Bluesbreakers and Fleetwood Mac purported to maintain and develop the blues traditions, in fact those traditions were rapidly dispersed and lost within what became 'rock.' Although often referenced in the same sentence as the blues, for many the extended solos of guitarists such as Eric Clapton - that admittedly hearten audiences worldwide - are a long way away from what blues really meant to achieve in the hearts and minds of its very first audiences.

All of which means that listeners should be suspicious of any group of twenty-somethings purporting to be a 'blues band.' Fortunately, for White Stripes fans, that suspicion can be allayed. Talking about the blues, Jack has often referred to his frustration with other members of his own musical generation, who, raised and influenced in the 1980s and 1990s, have never traced back the roots of the music they first grew to love. Like many older musicians, Jack discovered the blues through trawling back through liner notes of albums as already mentioned, but also via books such as Robert Palmer's seminal tome *Deep Blues,* to find the roots of the roots of the roots of the music he loved: a raw and energetic sound, appropriate for a new century where all semblance of authenticity appeared to bleed out of the international music scene. Frustrated by America's ever-forward march for greater and more technology, by a world in which any high-school kid can access recording facilities with hundreds of available tracks and samples to fill them without leaving his or her bedroom, Jack is a man for whom four tracks is probably enough, and eight a luxury.

Thus the band's first, eponymous album bears many influences. On *The White Stripes* there are shades of Hendrix, broad strokes of Led Zeppelin, even an echo (for the British ear) of Irish blues-rocker Rory Gallagher. But, in the sense that it utilises the format with a ferocity and economy of attack rare in contemporary rock, and also in that it broadens those brush strokes without losing its spirit, this is a blues album through and through.

From the start it is clear where this album is going. Ironically, given the constant spotlight that was placed on Jack, it is Meg's drumming that is at the core of what this band is about. Two bars of basic on-the-floor pounding introduce a raw, over-driven guitar phrase, soon picked up and thrown at a ferocious pace into the first verse. 'Jimmy The Exploder', with its hollered 'ho-ho-ho's and repeated delta guitar riff, is closer to the spirit of great blues men like Son House and Lightnin' Hopkins than any number of contemporary wealthy Texan session men who lend 'blues licks' to a myriad of AOR albums. What strikes immediately is the obvious and much-mooted lack of a bass guitar, so vital in the sound of a traditional rock band, but surplus to requirements (and generally not available) for early delta blues guitarists.

The guitar works equally hard in 'Stop Breaking Down,' a gritty, sweaty machine powering a careering engine of sound. Written by Robert Johnson, the mystical myth-making father of modern blues, the song was one of a handful of recordings by Johnson that informed blues and rock for decades to come. Jack's phrasing recalls 'Don't Bring Me Down,' by sixties British pseudo-Stones band the Pretty Things (which was covered on David Bowie's covers album *Pin-Ups* in the mid-1970s), a band themselves close to the heart of the blues renaissance of the early 1960s. But this is earthier stuff, closer to Johnson. A tambourine sprinkles a little lightness into Meg's heavy-duty drums, but Jack keeps the engine running with guitar motifs, including slide, that recall early electric blues riffs, and vocal whoops and hollers that legendary blues harp man Sonny Terry might have enjoyed. The ghost of Led Zeppelin inhabits the track too, White's vocals recalling Robert Plant throughout. Energy, fun, commitment and authenticity run through this track as it had through early Motown releases, classic T Rex vamps or the Who's early classics, and prove that - however dark - the blues can be fun.

'The Big Three Killed My Baby,' – as mentioned betraying White's distaste for the motor industry of hometown Detroit - and the Stones-influenced 'Suzy Lee,' follow in quick succession. 'The Big Three...' delivers a broadside attack on the modern car industry that puts profits before safety, culture or refinement. The band once played the track live on the Detroit PBS show 'Backstage Pass,' though the recording was not aired. With a grinning irony, the show was sponsored by General Motors!

Rich in Brian Jones-style slide guitar and 'Little Red Rooster'-era Mick Jagger vocals, 'Suzy Lee' is a hybrid of original Delta blues, 1960s revivalism and contemporary Detroit angst (Soledad Brothers' guitarist Johnny Walker plays second slide guitar on 'Suzy Lee' and, later, on 'I Fought Piranhas.'). On 'Sugar Never Tasted So Good', Jack breaks out the acoustic guitar, slowing the pace of the album for the first time. The song, even on disk, comes across very much as a *performance*, with the guitarist banging on the sound box of the guitar between phrases, and Meg alternating between silence, tambourine and drum kit throughout. The repeated lyrical lines - 'sugar never tasted...' etc - recall classic blues declamations, as do the Jagger-ish 'awrights' smattered throughout.

Kicking off in a minor key, 'Wasting My Time' again brings in later blues influences from across the Atlantic, with a little early Fleetwood Mac, Yardbirds and Them all evident, themselves vital to the Stooges-era Michigan music scene. What goes around comes around. This track is perhaps the most epigrammatic of White's lyrical offerings to date, reflecting the cyclical human condition: if a lover waits forever for an honest word, spends the time of loss looking back at his or her own actions, nevertheless the rivers flow and the waters keep on rising...

Riff-heavy 'Cannon' carries some Led Zep into a version of Son House's 'John The Revelator', a classic electric blues whose lyrics carry a traditional biblical theme. Many early blues bore a hymn-like significance, linking a traditional or biblical tale with a personal testament from the singer. Son House - to whom Jack White dedicated the album - lived the century of blues almost from end to end. It is a perfect choice of cover.

After 'Cannon' comes the dubious 'Astro', the eighth track on the album. Many listeners found its plodding riff and repetitive lyrics irritating - it lacks both the attack of earlier tracks and their lyrical clarity. Jack White has described 'Astro' as the thing you do in secret that "nobody knows about," but admits that until seconds before the recording was committed to tape it remained an instrumental, with no lyrics at all. The word 'astro' acts as an abstract retro symbol with implied references to those things beyond ourselves (the stars) about which we know so little and dream so much - fitting the concept of a hidden inner life well.

A wail of feedback introduces 'Broken Bricks,' a slap-happy punk thrash with excellent, crashing, heavy-on-the-cymbals drum work and the battering of a school-teacher's bell from Meg. Lyrically the song looks at a bleak landscape of urban desolation where lives continue amongst the decay of demolition (the song shares the lyric credit between Stephen Gillis and Jack White). The broken bricks, cyclone fence, caution tape and rust-coloured rain paint a sorry picture of where the object of the song first got herself kissed, where her father worked and where her brother first laid a punch on someone. Beneath the Stooges-lite swagger of the instrumentation, this is one of the most sensitive and evocative lyrics on the album.

The Stooges, John Lee Hooker and the Rolling Stones rear their heads on track ten, the bluesy 'When I Hear My Name.' The song mixes restrained drumming from Meg with blues guitar riffs on two guitars mixed through the same stereo channel from Jack. Lyrically simple, it nevertheless carries that haiku-like quality of many blues songs, expressing here the simple concept of - when faced with the facts of one's self, by name and by appearance - wishing to disappear from view. Like 'Cannon,' and elsewhere on the album, there runs throughout strong elements of self-loathing and violence.

'Do,' the next track, maintains this self-doubt and confusion. Slower, hanging on a funky beat punctuated by long instrumental silences while the singer declaims (often Dylan-like), 'Do' explores elements of the singer's life. In his relationship with his mother, his fan base, an encounter with a stranger and even within his own thoughts he finds deception, loss of faith and confidence and a lack of sincerity. Even the influence of his "idols" is questioned, as the more he listens to what they have to say to him the more they fade away. The title of the song is typically ironic - although entitled 'Do', it examines the things that the singer 'can't do.'

These songs bear common themes, and demonstrate the cause and the effect of Detroit's dissolution, a strong thematic under-current to much of The White Stripes world. Painted today as a city in decline, Detroit's history is actually very much of a cyclical city, always somewhere in the eternal circle of decline or rebirth. While every Motown may fade away, some new revolution may be around the next corner. But amidst the urban chaos of 'Broken Bricks' lie the broken characters of 'When I Hear My Name' and 'Do,' unable to relate to themselves, the city and the people around them. Whether this urban landscape is Detroit, Los Angeles, London or Berlin, the picture that The White Stripes paint of civil decay is as disturbing as any from the hip-hop streets of America, and while architects and property magnates may benefit from the constant changing of our urban environments, the people who live there only suffer.

'Screwdriver' is the fictionalised account of an attempt to mug Jack White, a vicious, authentic electric blues riff supporting a nasal, rancorous vocal. As the song progresses, Jack's voice can't decide between Marc Bolan or John Lee Hooker, so resorts to a crazed, high-register shout. But away from the vocal mannerism, it's the guitar that makes this song work: it plays on a riff the likes of which was often heard in the 1960s work of English guitarists like Peter Green and Eric Clapton, but they never achieved the venom and attack registered here.

Dylan's original version of 'One More Cup Of Coffee' is a mystical trip into the great man's cracked psyche, often delivered live in a mean, accusatory voice, brooding with Dylan's paranoid suspicion. Jack White loses none of these features, but first and foremost his version is *angry*. Opening up with cautious, understated minor-key guitar reminiscent of Dylan's own, Meg gives Jack's vocals (and this is a song that really needs singing!) room to move amongst simple on-the-floor drumming and lengthy silences that themselves accentuate the guitar's simplicity. Touches of Steve Winwood-style 1960s organ, introduced in the second verse, compliment the track well: this is grand, expository and symbolic music, and illustrates well the versatility of The White Stripes. Where at a cursory listen the non-fan may find their restrictive arrangements repetitive and their music one-dimensional, they demonstrate here a clarity of vision and ambition in taking on a Dylan song rarely covered by others and intensely personal in its vision. Cunningly, to an older generation, the recording also proves that The White Stripes are a bona fide outfit that has paid their musical dues. Whether smart marketing or authentic homage, the inclusion of 'One More Cup Of Coffee' was a masterstroke.

'Little People' takes the listener into the child-like world of the Stripes, where lyrics of innocents abroad cut against the rusty nails of Jack's guitar. The song is a series of snapshots of children in a variety of scenarios - boy with a spider, girl with a tiger on her bed, boy with nothing on his mind etc. The repeated refrain "hello", with Meg's stabbing cymbal crashes on each beat, suggests a questioning of each vaguely surreal image, but within the context of Jack's lyrics as a whole, inevitably the listener is drawn to the last line about a little boy with nothing on his mind. Are these quasi-blues lyrics nothing more than sounds to accompany the heavy riff of the song? If the little boy of the last verse turned out to be Jack, would the previous lines only have been created to fill that nothingness? At times it seems that Jack deliberately takes the central meaning out of a song, leaving a doughnut-shaped concept where the listener is asked to insert his or her own 'meaning' into the central blank space. Perhaps the 'meaning' of the series of images here is intended to be created within the listener's imagination?

They may not like it, but the Stripes drip Zeppelin. Whether this is intentional or an inevitable result of their sharing the same influences and inspirations (in which case they will inevitably sometimes meet at the same crossroads), 'Slicker Drips' could have come out of the Page and Plant songbook. No bad thing - this is a rollercoaster electric blues that takes 'Whole Lotta Love' several miles further down the tracks. Interspersing some rich open-string John Lee Hooker guitar lines with the power chords of a heavy duty band, Meg's drumming is ferocious - she's no body-builder, but she can hit the beat harder than many a tattooed metal-head.

Jack's rollicking piano chords form the basis of 'St James Infirmary Blues', a popular standard for many performers over decades. Jack has spoken at length about his love for 'older' musical formats, the simplicity of not just blues but of the works of writers such as Cole Porter and George Gershwin. Theirs was an often elegant musical simplicity, apparently at odds with The White Stripes' inelegant garage thrash, but in White's song-writing armoury there is a similar economy of technique: *don't use thirty words where five will do, but if you can say it more clearly with a guitar lick than a rhyme, then let the instrument do the talking.* On this cover song, Jack rolls the piano chords over and over (it's good to hear a piano that sounds as though it is made of wood and wire), and his vocal performance is theatrical, recalling early Tom Waits or Nick Cave, histrionic story-tellers of the first order. Adding to the authentic piano sound, he finishes the song off with a theatrical swipe up the exposed strings of the instrument: as elsewhere on White Stripes albums, there is often a tangible sense of 'performance' at work, a feeling that while always in touch with the roots of their own music, the pair are forever aware of the listening audience at the end of the line, and of their desire to be *entertained.*

Question: how do you wind up an album with so much life, such a variety of sounds and musical journeys? Answer: roll out the dirtiest slide guitar blues you can muster and confuse the hell out of anyone who takes the trouble to pay attention! 'I Fought Piranhas' beats the living daylights out of any contemporary blues performance: Jack may or may not be the best guitarist of his generation (depending on the listener's own point of view), but unlike many so-called 'better' guitarists, he understands more about how a blues guitar should *feel* than anyone else, and blues is all about *feel.* Having said that, few listeners could figure out what the lyrics to 'I Fought Piranhas' were all about!

The White Stripes is a remarkable debut. Three albums later into their career, it was proved to be probably not their best, but as a debut it is a stunning achievement from a band so steeped in the history of rock and blues and yet so very much themselves, contemporary and together. As a guitar-player, writer and vocalist Jack White is versatile, ambitious and above all has a wonderful understanding of *what a guitar is for.* Meg too understands her role entirely. Her drumming is articulate, economical and on every single track lands exactly where it ought to be in the mix.

And they rock...

The cover of the debut album was designed by the multi-skilled Patti and Andy of Flying Bomb, another example of how intertwined the numerous players in the Detroit scene had become. Their design services came under the name Ballistic Design and were renowned for their part-Jamie Reid, part-fifties pop art designs – other bands who have used them include The Hentchmen, Blowtops and Bantam Rooster. It was during this period that Andy got to know Jack much better. "He started dropping by a lot, but he kinda does that. He finds somebody and just starts hanging out with them for a long time.

Meg's real nice although I never really talked to her a lot. She'd come over occasionally for a barbecue or something like that, she was really nice, she didn't really take part in a lot of things. She's a little more quiet, refrained."

From their first album onwards, The White Stripes have maintained a cool, consistent and detached style in their cover artwork. The first album's sleeve frames three shots of Meg and Jack as though consecutively shot on a single role of film. The photos were taken by Ko Melina Zydeco (spelt with a 'k' in the credits), vocalist, drummer, percussionist and bassist in Detroit bands Ko & The Knockouts (who were later recorded and produced by Mr Jack White), the Breakdowns and the Come Ons. The impact is visually immediate: this is a band to look at as well as to listen to.

White lettering on a red background, red and white clothing against a vertical red surface and a red and white peppermint candy flood the senses with... red. The back cover, expanding the format with a different angle on a similar pair of shots, cements the image: "You don't know The White Stripes? - Well... they look like *this!"*

Like a pair of indie refugees, Jack and Meg appear not only impassive but unconnected: all that links them visually in the photos is a sense of design - abstraction not emotion. The inner sleeve displays a warmer side - the couple (plus the candy) are posed against white stripes on red backgrounds, and - at least from Meg - there are smiles.

Against these images, the lyric sheets of five of the album's songs are presented in old-fashioned, typewriter-like format, like scripts from a movie from which the still images could have been taken. And there's some text, uncredited but presumably from Jack. It recalls Jack Kerouac's punctuation-free, stream of consciousness, written-in-one-session manuscript for *On The Road,* the classic beat novel of the late 1940s, and concerns issues raised on the albums songs, in particular the concept of innocence and the loss/embracement of childhood – a dichotomy at the very heart of the band.

The liner notes thank God in the first instance, family in the second, and a list of associates thirdly. Repeating the theme of the peppermint candy on the disk itself, the image occupies the entire circle of the CD. There is no text to identify the band or the album. Confident of their visual integrity even by this first album, the Stripes have already defined their profile sufficiently to dispense with words.

And here, in a nutshell of economical and effective design, is the first manifesto of The White Stripes: abstraction; emotional distance (although Jack's songs are highly emotional in style, in content he keeps a space between his 'self' and the 'meaning' of his songs); visual immediacy; lyricism; confidence; innocence and its loss; boy/girl; red/white; art/pop; Jack/Meg. It is, in many ways, a perfect debut album sleeve.

The small amount of press solicited by the first album was generally positive, with this summary from writer Grant Cogswell being the most choice appraisal: "*The White* Stripes is a shock to the system, a blast from a fire hose of primal punk blues, comparable in its haunting singularity and delicious goth hysteria to the Cramps' classic first EP. On *The White Stripes*, Jack and Meg White are possessed by a fusion of electric blues and the binary frenzy of echoplexed two-chord punk, and they rule."

So all, it seemed, was going well. There was however, one fairly major problem. Just after the first album sessions were completed, Jack and Meg had split up.

CHAPTER 9

"You should try everything once, except incest and folk-dancing."

Sir Arnold Bax

"She walked out of the studio, pretty much left him," relates Andy of Flying Bomb. "They'd got married pretty young. Jack would be coming over and saying, 'Oh, you know, we're getting divorced... Meg's left me.' I guess he was a little bummed about it. We had to go through all the pictures on the record sleeve artwork to take out all the wedding rings. That was kinda entertaining!"

The relationship ended just before The Blowout Festival organised by alternative entertainment weekly magazine *Metro Times*. In light of their recent split, Meg was initially not going to play this show and Jack even spoke with another drummer about standing in, but at the last minute Meg was confirmed on the drum stool. The pair would eventually get divorced in 2000.

Being unable to share a marital home has not got in the way of many classic bands – turbulent relationships can be found at the heart of Fleetwood Mac and Abba for example. With The White Stripes just beginning to gather some momentum, many observers thought this split would mean a certain premature end to a promising career. Not so. It soon became apparent that the severance of the union in marriage would have no lasting effect on their partnership within The White Stripes. "Next thing, all I heard from Jack," continues Andy of Flying Bomb, "was that Meg was still real interested in the band still... she really liked doing it. She wanted to do it some more and I think (their circumstances) really changed things a lot, because before she'd just kinda followed what he played. She was a little more in control afterwards. I think that was a real key point for her. And her drumming became much harder, a lot more powerful. She definitely had a lot more confidence later.

The gigs at that time were great. They'd be coming out and singing the same songs but always doing each track slightly differently. Lots of improv, it was always amazing. They played The Gold Dollar one night and Jack had a very sore throat, he was real sick. He screamed the whole show, amazing!"

Graff was also not surprised when they continued to play together: "They don't spend that much time together other than the musical time. Besides, there are lots of examples of rock 'n' roll creative teams that stayed together creatively after a relationship split."

Around this time, Andy felt the White Stripes were really starting to show massive potential: "There was a point where you'd go see them play and certain songs would thrill you. At the same time, for some people I think The White Stripes became very much a love/hate thing. We'd first seen this when we put out that Christmas record. I was shocked at which people liked it and which people didn't - the latter really hated it yet other people, who I would never think in a million years would be into it, would be hugely excited. At that point, we started noticing there was definitely something interesting there that was clicking, that was really cool. It was definitely a step up."

Gary Graff agrees: "That first album was actually better than anybody expected. More people started seeing them live too, but for me it was the songwriting, these were good songs. I started to think, 'Right, okay, something's happening here,' plus there was the fact that he was always a real interesting guitar player. *The White Stripes* was really a bit of a wake up call, they're pulling something off here."

By the end of 1999, with the debut album out, his various other projects on the back-burner and the split with Meg successfully negotiated, Jack's full focus was on The White Stripes. They continued gigging relentlessly, although at times they found this hard. Bobby Harlow, vocalist with the Go told Brian McCollum how, "it was tough for (The White Stripes) at first. People saw it as half a band. When you've got a night full of five-piece bands, and then you've got a drummer and guitar player, it's hard to get a promoter to take you seriously. Jack was bummed out: 'We can't headline, we can't get anything. We're a two-piece and nobody takes us seriously.'" Nonetheless, the growing energy at their live shows of the period was perhaps best shown during a tour with Pavement and Sleater Kinney in the fall of that year.

These shows had a lasting effect on Jack. "There were 800 people there," recalls Ben Blackwell of the Pavement date he saw the Stripes on, at the Recher Theater in Towson, "by far the biggest crowd they had ever played in front of. They were supposed to play a half-hour set or something, but because they were so nervous they played it super fast and did it in twenty minutes!" The shows got bigger and Jack and Meg both seemed taken aback by the progress. "I think the Pavement gigs really helped," opines Jim Diamond. Those were the first biggest shows they really played. I remember them saying, 'Oh my God we've played in front of 2,000 people!"

Yet, at the end of the tour the duo had not made enough money to even cover their meagre expenses, but Pavement very kindly did that for them. Meanwhile, back in Detroit, news of these shows and the spreading gospel of the debut album was starting to whip up considerable interest in the band.

"They were just another Detroit band that got on Sympathy which seemed like no great feat," Mick Collins told me. "That was cool but then they went on tour with Pavement and Sleater Kinney and were gone for like three months and when they came back it seemed like suddenly they were famous. I don't know quite how that happened but I am damn sure I wish I could get some of it!"

In light of The White Stripes' huge global success and the quality of other bands coming out of Detroit, the city has become known for this latest revival in garage rock-style music. However, in the mid-to-late 1990s, there were other cells of music festering in Detroit, most notably the Kid Rock/Eminem phenomenon and the continued evolution of the techno scene.

Both Kid Rock and Eminem had taken a white boy slant on the hip-hop genre and fused it with elements of rock and pop to create multi-platinum selling profiles. Initially, Kid Rock was the biggest of the two artists - strippers, green haired DJs, basement parties, on-the-road excess, studio brilliance and media frenzies across Rock's ten year career marked him out in an era when God-fearing sugary pop seems to rule the music world. Kid Rock's openly self-indulgent hedonism and brutal genre-hopping music proved to be an irresistible return to the oldest excesses of rock 'n' roll, seen at its most inspirational with the hit album *Devil Without A Cause*.

Eminem, Marshall Mathers, Slim Shady brought up the rear and leap-frogged over every other rap artist at the turn of the Millennium to become the biggest solo star in the world. His breath-taking rhymes and lyrical skills, blended with ultra-cool associations with the likes of Dr Dre, filled both his debut album and his record-breaking follow-up, *The Marshall Mathers LP*, with some of the most provocative, lyrically brilliant and musically stunning material of recent times. The intense spotlight on his own personal life constantly competed with the extreme world of his infamous character Slim Shady. His life was, indeed, true theater - his music was pure genius. Both were examined in the semi-autobiographical smash movie, *Eight Mile*, which once more threw the media focus back on Detroit.

Likewise, albeit to a more underground public, techno - the last major movement to come out of Detroit was born of the continued decline in the city's economic fortunes through the 1970s and 1980s. Although the history of the city demonstrates a continual cycle of generation, decline and re-generation, the down-turn in the industrial sectors of the economy left gaping holes in downtown Detroit, filled as always by some of the poorest sections of the community. Once again, the concepts of mass-production, technological advance and urbanism were to shape the new culture just had they had for Motown. The technological developments of rap music in some sense showed the way - the ability to cut and paste James Brown or Led Zeppelin onto contemporary beats carried much of the same sense of technological revolution within black music as did techno - but where rap and hip-hop proclaim emotions as loud as any soul or gospel record, techno - with its dependence upon non-human sources - created a cool emotional distance between the listener/dancer and the music.

Techno as a musical format gained worldwide recognition after its development in Europe - particularly in Belgium and in cities of the UK such as Sheffield, also industrial centres left behind in the economic changes of the time. The speed with which the new ecstasy-fuelled dance clubs of the UK had embraced Chicago house music was dramatic, and in looking for the next inspiration, record company executives recognised in Detroit's techno scene a new, versatile and high energy dance format that would indeed become a world-wide club phenomenon.

It was the work of a handful of Detroiters who created the original techno buzz. Vietnam vet Richard Davies (known as '30370') teamed up with Juan Atkins, and with one of the first Roland sequencers began making their own electronic music. 'Alleys of Your Mind', their first release, sold more than 12,000 copies in and around the Detroit area, and quickly established them as happening. As Cybotron, Atkins and 3070 developed a whole concept for extending the Techno ideal, and by the mid-1980s, tracks such as 'Techno City,' 'Clear' and 'R-9' had established the format that so neatly encapsulate the spirit of post-industrial Detroit, increasingly devoid of a soul that the sophisticated new music seemed to be searching for.

Virgin Records funded the first commercial 'exploration' of Detroit's new music, and the 12-track album *Techno! The New Dance School of Detroit* was the spark that lit the flame that burned through the coming years of British and European pop, developing dance music from its side-line role in British music to becoming, alongside hip-hop, the single most popular format for CD sales. The rebirth of European holiday destinations such as Ibiza as wild-time-disco-heaven destinations led to a huge development on the back of house and techno, as the movements splintered, combined, re-structured into a myriad of different formats - ambient house and ambient techno, techno hardcore and so on. From its original Detroit roots, techno was heavily present amongst the releases of Aphex Twin, Orbital and the Orb, and became integral to the e-generation. In the twenty-first century it remains one of Detroit's most accessible gifts to the world.

And yet, none of this mattered to The White Stripes or indeed any of the other regulars at The Gold Dollar. Despite their proximity to the streets where this all happened for Rock, Eminem and the techno geniuses, I have found no single personality from the scene associated with The White Stripes who has any knowledge or contact with these parallel environments. "I don't know any of those people today and I never did," explained Jim Diamond. "That was a totally different thing. We were all pretty much downtown Detroit people and they were for the most part out in the suburbs."

Matt Smith of Outrageous Cherry has this to say on the subject: "The rock scene, the techno scene and the rap scene are all fairly separate. The techno guys - I think those guys are socially like Kraftwerk! There's a little cross over here and there but not much. There are people in Detroit who are attracted to the whole diversity of it and don't want to see it narrowly defined, but then there's other people that are just really caught up in their own thing."

For his part, Jack is bored of having to explain this and when questioned about Eminem or Kid Rock in interviews has taken to just blankly saying, "No comment". Some journalists have perceptively pointed out the lyrical certain similarities between some of Eminem's more personal songs and those of The White Stripes, but the (rather tenuous) likeness is put down by Jack to no more than a coincidence, just artists writing about life.

The short length of time it took The White Stripes to record their debut album was mirrored by the speed with which they began work on the follow-up. The single which preceded the second album was 'Hello Operator', just over 150 seconds of raucous, electrifying White Stripes noise. Perhaps more notable was the B-side which was their own unbelievable take on Dolly Parton's country standard, 'Jolene'. This eyebrow-raising cover would go on to be a live staple in the Stripes increasingly feverish gigging career. The original pressing was a picture disc that naturally now commands a high premium among circles of people with nothing better to do.

As an aside, Jack is very particular about the duo's selection of covers, as he explained in to the web magazine *Launch*: "We've never covered a song simply because it would be cool or because we'd seem really obscure for doing so. Certain circles of musicians will all get involved with the same record at the same time and suddenly it will be cool to like the Kinks' *Village Green Preservation Society* for a month. But why didn't people feel that way three years ago? I've always hated the whole idea of record collectors who are obsessed with how obscure something is. Usually when somebody brings up something obscure, I assume it's not very good, because, if it was, I would have heard it already. Record collectors are collecting. They're not really listening to music."

For this second album, the aforementioned parameters were loosened a little although with Jack recording much of the material at home the speed and cost remained very tightly controlled. Jim Diamond was in the mixing/co-production chair again and had this to say to me about the project: "Jack recorded it at his home, which is only about ten minutes away from my studio. Then we mixed it here. I didn't really spend any time with Meg on that one. Jack had an eight-track analogue machine and I had the same thing here. He wanted to take more time because, as I mentioned earlier, we used up a lot of hours doing multiple takes and things on the first record. He thought, 'Well, I could record it at home - guitar and drums and a bit of vocal - in our free time and then we can go over to Jim's and mix it together.'"

This was not ideal from Jim Diamond's point of view, but he was pleased to be working with Jack and Meg again nonetheless: "I prefer to work on a project from the start, not just be employed to mix the recording. This is especially the case if it is a home recording like this, where the standards might not ideally be what I would like. I like to be involved in the production of the music from the start, working with the artist from the beginning on a recording."

In retrospect, this reservation was something that Jack later agreed with himself. "(The second album) was a big thing for me. To record at home was a bad idea," he told *X-Ray*. "There were too many distractions - the phone ringing and all that jazz. And people knocking on the door. We even had some drunk guy walked in to the house off the street while we were recording 'Death Letter'... he'd just wandered in because he'd heard us playing."

Jack also played a pivotal role in the mixing of the album once it was taken out of Third Man and into Jim's Ghetto Records. "Jack and I mixed it. It's not his job to be a recording engineer and I would definitely do things differently than he would, *but* he had pretty limited means at that point, his eight-track and a few microphones only. I did whatever I could to make it sound as good as possible. But again this was not a lengthy project. I don't know how much time Jack and Meg spent recording that at home, but my mixing bill for that second album was only about $600."

From day one, The White Stripes have been about style. Not necessarily in the Kate Moss sense of fashion and elegance, but certainly in terms of understanding the 'one single message' concept of marketing. 'The White Stripes? - they're the couple in red and white, yeah?' It's a clear message, but the music carries its own clarity beyond the visuals. The Stripes have 'style,' so it was no great surprise that their second album should be called (in Dutch) 'the style.'

The record was to be called *De Stijl*, named after the early twentieth century Dutch abstract art movement led by Gerrit Rietveld and Piet Mondrian, based on simplistic ideas such as colours and vertical and horizontal lines. This work typified the march towards abstraction through the post-impressionist years of the new century. It was all about back-to-basics in design. The movement's style is clearly relevant to the Stripes' own design concept: clear, bold rectangles of pure, usually primary colour, separated into planes of space by straight black lines. It is a logical step to move from the primarily red, black and white of the first album sleeve to the Mondrian-inspired abstractions of the second.

"We thought it went pretty well with what we do," said Jack. He also said, "they had to abandon (the art movement) because they couldn't get it any simpler than it was. It was a question of how simple should The White Stripes be, what's out of bounds for us, and what are we supposed to be doing with this band?" (they were, of course, not the first band to draw inspiration from art movements – for example, seminal indie

Early Days
Top Left Playing guitar with 'The Go' *Top Right* The infamous Gold
Dollar *Centre Right* 'The Go' *Bottom* Early 'White Stripes'

Influences
Clockwise from Top Left Charlie
Patton, Robert Johnson, Bob Dylan,
Led Zeppelin

Local Heros
Clockwise from Top Left MC5,
The Dirtbombs, The Gories,
Iggy Pop

Press Darlings

treasures Mega City Four used artwork from Hieronymous Bosch for their album *Sebastopol Road*).

If in some way the album *De Stijl* is an art show, then the exhibits on its walls show a greater variety of writing style than the first album, dubbed by one critic as "minimum R&B" (as opposed to the "maximum R&B" of the Who). Jack spoke of his desire to flesh out the basics of the first album, but to avoid the excesses of such devices as string arrangements. In other words, take the core of album one and imagine how it could be even better on album two.

The comparisons between Mondrian's art and the Stripes music is as valid as that linking their visual appeal. Like the work of the modernist painters who followed Mondrian, Jack and Meg have designed a music that fits neatly within their own concept, is typified by unsophisticated construction that - when fitted together well - is uniquely powerful. Their 'lines' of communication via the music (like the black lines of Mondrian's paintings) are clear and easily followed - we don't have to work too hard to understand the songs here, yet they are infinitely rewarding. Mondrian's work easily fits the classroom wall, explains modern art to children, yet it commands huge prices from the art establishment. So Jack and Meg's corny school kid songs and ragged, heavy blues are often gloriously simple expressions of emotion yet they receive the plaudits of the most discerning critics.

Jack has often discussed song-writing and in particular the dubious business of writing 'catchy' songs - a role he finds difficult yet interesting. On 'You're Pretty Good Looking (For A Girl),' the opening track of *De Stijl*, he seems to have had no difficulty finding more hooks than in the dressing room of the Detroit Tigers. One of the catchiest of all The White Stripes' songs, and compared by many listeners to the Kinks, there is a distinctive English smirk in the 'o-yeah' verses that could be Merseybeat, could be the Hollies, but is most reminiscent of Pete Townsend at his poppiest best – shades of 'I'm A Boy'/'Pictures Of Lily'-era Who songs. The descending guitar that leads into the Beatle-ish middle eight is drum-skin tight, and on first listening it was really refreshing to hear a band able to cram so much good material into less than two-minutes worth of music.

The twin guitars and drums of the single *Hello Operator* are supplemented by the harmonica of John Szymanski, Detroit bass player with bands such as the Hentchmen, Detroit Cobras and the Paybacks. From the opening pop of '… Pretty Good Looking', listeners to the new Stripes album are immediately transported back to the delta blues. Meg counts neatly in square fours, and Jack's vocals are cocksure, belligerent and looking for a fight. Track three stays in the delta for another slide blues. 'Little Bird' is a more traditional lyric, a mix of horny misogyny and bible-preaching bragadoccio. It's clear that the second album has lost none of the respect for traditional urban blues so evident on the first.

The album is dedicated to Blind Willie McTell, the multi-talented blind guitarist from Georgia, whose recordings still represent an enormous legacy in American popular culture. McTell (1901-1959, who recorded under several different names to avoid contractual confusion, thereby confusing biographers for years to come!) developed an intricate style on the twelve-string guitar, mixing finger-picking and slide to create a delicate, rhythmic sound, and his likewise high-register, quavering voice was loaded with emotion. Blind Willie - a lifelong inspiration to Bob Dylan - is certainly amongst the most influential of blues guitarists, but as a story-teller he was almost as influential on later song-writers, his narrative style conversational and approachable.

There's an element of Blind Willie in the picked/slide verses of 'Little Bird,' but the flavour is much more of the later, urban blues of Lightnin' Hopkins. Track four 'Apple Blossom,' however, re-introduces a gentler side of the band in Jack's acoustic guitar and piano. As with 'St James Infirmary Blues' and other previously released tracks, it is again good to hear a piano that really sounds *like a piano* on this Ray Davies-ish track. Many of the White Stripes contemporaries use the piano as an instrument to add substance to an otherwise weak sound, thereby often losing the actual sonics of the instrument within the mix. However, here, the piano is used specifically and deliberately as a melodic lead. Amongst their peers, perhaps Coldplay is the finest example of a band using the piano in this way. It was refreshing to see the White Stripes – a band which after all are rooted in the blues – using the piano in thus. Straightforward strumming and tambourine from Meg ease the song in gently, and it picks up pace throughout. A favourite among fans, 'Apple Blossom' is a Jack White song that teeters on the brink of irony yet retains a refreshing innocence.

'I'm Bound To Pack It Up' continues the easier-listening theme. Continuing to define an already more varied album than its predecessor, 'I'm Bound...' includes Jack on upright bass and the clear, punchy violin of Paul Henry Ossy. Jack's vocals are again reminiscent of Paul McCartney at his rural best (the track most reminds the listener of

'Mother Nature's Son' from The Beatles' *White Album*), while Ossy's violin, free of reverb or any other sweetening device, adds melodic touches throughout. Easier listening it may appear to be, but the lyrics represent a sorry scene: the singer leaves a worn-out relationship, joining a bus-load of runaways looking for another way as his ex-lover sits silently by the telephone.

Son House's 'Death Letter' pulls no punches. We're back in the deep waters of the blues with "ten thousand people standing on the burial ground." Recorded by a number of artists including Blind Willie Johnson and, in 2003, John Mellancamp, this is a dark number indeed, on which Jack's open-string guitar playing and slide are relentless. As the song progresses, Jack and Meg speed up the pace considerably, only to halt and drop back to the original slower tempo.

Another recurrent theme - the feckless schoolboy lost in the mechanics of early love - recurs in 'Sister, Do You Know My Name?' This is a slow burner - softly-sung lyrics from Jack, patient silences from Meg and bluesy, fat guitar phrases build up to an unexpectedly positive conclusion - this time there's no interfering mother, no hassle: it just might work out!

The brilliantly-titled 'Truth Doesn't Make A Noise', is about how victims often cannot speak the truth, but how their silence speaks the bigger truth. Opening on minor-chord acoustic guitar (almost a sibling of *The White Stripes'* 'One More Cup Of Coffee,') and punctuated with grand piano chords, the track is in part-cinematic ham and part-desperate yearning, a Rolling Stones demo in which Ian Stewart turned up on piano while Keith and Bill stayed home. Lyrically this is one of Jack's most delicate songs - he has a genuinely tender side to his songwriting that is sometimes lost beneath the swaggering guitar and pounding drums. White has an economy with words that leaves *in* just enough meaning to point the way to understanding, yet leaves *out* just enough meaning to make sure that the listener/reader - if they take the time - creates his or her own song out of the Stripes' own material. So it is here - is the subject of the song dead? Disabled? Handicapped? Or merely unloved? It isn't clear from the lyric, but we understand the point: listen to what she is telling *you* to do, even if she isn't saying anything.

'A Boy's Best Friend,' the ninth track on *De Stijl* is perhaps the albums first weak spot. A slow, self-pitying contemporary slide blues, it simply doesn't go anywhere. Fortunately the next track, the Bolan-boogie-styled 'Let's Build A Home' gets further in its first minute (half of which is taken up by a recording of a small boy reciting poetry or song lyrics), replete with insane whoops and hollers from Jack, a series of firework fretboard tricks and 'get-the-car-we're-leaving' drumming from Meg. Somewhere in the lyrics there's a bit about setting up home together, building a house, getting it together, but - let's face it - this song is for jumping around to.

You can jump around to 'Jumble, Jumble' too, after the clip from French-language radio gets out of the way, in a Chuck Berry kind of way. The album draws towards its close with the disappointing, again self-pitying 'Why Can't You Be Nicer To Me?', saved by Meg's changes of pace and distorted violin from Paul Henry Ossy.

Country blues rears its acoustic head again for a couple of minutes again on 'Your Southern Can Is Mine,' the album's last track. A Blind Willie McTell song, this is a style of blues quite different from the electric blues that the Stripes are readily associated with. The track tails the album off well, with a little snippet of recorded conversation from Willie closing the show, but in general the album disappoints after 'Truth Doesn't Make A Noise.' More acoustic than the first album, perhaps more ambitious in its aims, there is too much variation in pace and the crash-and-burn velocity of *The White Stripes* is sacrificed for songs sometimes too whimsical to really hit home.

Drawing on an art movement inevitably makes the album artwork for *De Stijl* fascinating. The cover shows Jack and Meg standing within a modernist construction of flat planes of red and white, linked with straight black lines and the white clothing (but for Jack's red brothel-creepers) of the band members. Immediately we are back in the red and white world abstracted for the first album.

Images throughout the insert booklet include artwork from neo-plasticist Dutch architect Gerry Rietveld, author, curator and academic Paul Overy and modernist artists Theo Van Doesberg (founder of *De Stijl* magazine), Georges Vantongerloo and the Hungarian-born Vilmos Huszar. Amongst these are shots of Jack and Meg in various poses in the corner of a modernist room, with Meg's candy-striped bass drum, Jack's red and white guitar, and a fabulous customised Leslie speaker cabinet containing a two-speed revolving peppermint.

As on the artwork for *The White Stripes,* the photography was by another fellow Detroit band member-cum-photographer, Ewolf (Eric Wheeler), late of the Dirtbombs and Detroit City Council. Posed almost like modernist constructions themselves, Jack and Meg are again impassive in their poses, enjoying their roles as works of art within the exhibition that is the *De Stijl* sleeve. More lyrics are posted than previously, and again there is a manifesto (again, it is uncredited): breaking the rules of excess to acknowledge the beauty of simple things is the recommended route towards achieving beauty itself.

The De Stijl concept suits the band well: it proposes a design brief based on two-dimensional, anti-decorative images. De Stijl was economical and functional, anti-decorative in the sense that colour was not an adornment, but an essence of the design itself. Does this sound familiar? Function? Economy? Non-decorative? These are concepts at the core of The White Stripes' music, not just their sense of visual style. To blend the visual image of the band and their raison d'etre as musicians via an art movement that bears a synergy with both is a remarkably smart feat. The question was – particularly in light of the album's weaker spots – would anyone else agree?

CHAPTER 10

"One guitar player has an orchestra in his hands."

Jeff Buckley

At this point, The White Stripes had no publicist and no agent. Despite this, on its June 2000 release (exactly one year after their first album) *De Stijl* managed to get decent coverage in a modest amount of magazines, most notably a review in *Rolling Stone*. Once again a result of Jack White's focus and drive. That magazine said, "Feisty and clever, full of scuzzy garage rock. Meg White's drumming is so minimal that it's almost funny: It forces a smile because, like everything about The White Stripes, it proves that you don't need bombast to make a blues explosion."

There were some detractors - Grant Cogswell, who had so liked their debut album, was less convinced this time around. "Unfortunately the change from their debut's approach - which seemed as basic and elemental as could be with its caveman drums and loud guitar - is to go acoustic in large part, add other instrumentation, and pull away the mask of attitude and sex which made the first record so engaging... its songs are weaker than its predecessor's by a good deal."

Although the commercial impact of *De Stijl* was very limited indeed (on its release in the UK, *De Stijl* sold just over six hundred copies), it was after its release - with all the accompanying acclaim - that local people on the Detroit scene began to realise that Jack and Meg's star was very much in the ascendancy. Douglas Comombe, a photographer with local alternative entertainment magazine *Metro Times* said this was when he realised something big was happening: "With all the hype about The White Stripes, I think people (were) overlooking what great people Jack and Meg are. They're kind, friendly modest..." he later told *NME*, "(but) by the *De Stijl* release show, I could tell they were getting big. Lots of people who wouldn't be caught dead at The Gold Dollar were there - many suburbanites are scared of downtown Detroit. I knew they were on their way and I was happy for them. It was nice to see talent get its due."

There were, inevitably, a growing clique of detractors. Surge Joebot was still mystified at some of the sniping about this hard-earned success: "When *De Stijl* was reviewed in *Rolling Stone*, a lot of people were like, 'How come they're in R*olling Stone* instead of us?' And it's like, 'You shithead, because of *this* you probably *will* be in *Rolling Stone*. Just give it time.'"

While reports of very early shows suggest that the dynamism and chemistry between Jack and Meg on stage carried them through the gigs against a backdrop of occasionally less-than-perfect technical performances (particularly Meg), it is clear that The White Stripes were a hard gigging band from day one. Some observers attribute their prolific live schedules for lifting them above the myriad of Detroit bands, although it has to be said that the scene was generally one that revolved almost entirely around live shows.

As with his studio approach, Jack's live set-up was and remains somewhat rudimentary, something that Jim Diamond appreciates: "Jack's got all the same stuff as when I first saw them, he's not got too elaborate at all. Yet the live show has improved so much, they're great live now because they've played together so much." In the aftermath of the second album, the White Stripes already hectic touring schedules were intensified and with great effect.

What would turn out to be the band's last single for Sympathy For The Record Industry, the superb *'Lord Send Me An Angel'*, was released at this time too. As with Parton's 'Jolene', here the Stripes re-invent a classic, this time Blind Willie McTell's formerly acoustic blues, which is filtered through Jack's peculiar Stripes guitar into a festering masterpiece. The B-side is a remix of 'You're Pretty Good Looking...' with an odd, robotic-vocal effect (available as yet another red seven inch vinyl too!)

Most bands would be happy to work their way steadily through the growing number of live and media commitments that The White Stripes gathering momentum had created. Not so Jack and Meg White. They seemed to be constantly at work. During this period, The White Stripes also released their first and only split single, with former Gories luminary Mick Collins' Dirtbombs. Oddly enough given its latter-day (record collectors) value, the single actually came free with a pinball fanzine called *Multiball* (Jack is a pinball fan). The riffing frenzy is complemented by a spoken-word tale of a disastrous date at a bowling alley, a track so cool that *NME* called it "a lost White Stripes classic."

They also took the time to contribute versions of three Captain Beefheart tracks to the December 2000 Sub Pop Singles Club, namely 'Party Of Special Things To Do', 'China Pig' and 'Ashtray Heart'. This release was pressed up in an edition of 1300 all in candy cane-style red and white swirls.

In early 2001, Jack masterminded a compilation album called *The Sympathetic Sounds Of Detroit* (released in April). With interest in the city's burgeoning garage rock-style scene blossoming, Sympathy For The Record Industry felt this record would be a good way to capitalise on that attention and also to present a comprehensive selection of some of Detroit's finest bands. The idea was for Jack White to produce the record and each band would play on the same drum kit, guitar amps and microphones in the same room. Jim Diamond mixed the album once it had been captured by Jack on tape.

The Hentchmen were one of the bands chosen and Johnny of that act has this to say about this record: "Actually he recorded everything up in his attic at his house. The thing about the record is every sound was recorded in that room. We did it real quick you know. Ours was done in one evening. I think he set it up to do one band per night going in there. So perhaps it took a couple of weeks to get it all together. It was kind of his show. He kind of knows how we like to sound, he respected the way we like to sound."

Alongside The White Stripes and the Hentchmen were a host of fabulous Detroit bands including the Dirtbombs, the Detroit Cobras, the Von Bondies and the Soledad Brothers. For their part, The White Stripes contributed two tracks: the twenty-two second slither called 'Buzzard Blues' and 'Red Death At 6:14', a truly ferocious garage rock onslaught (complete with melodic backing vocals from Meg). The bands managed to largely sound different despite the restriction of having to use the same kit and equipment, making this album an essential document for anyone interested in this generation of Detroit guitar bands.

While the *Sympathetic Sounds* album was almost an official nod to the scene's increasing world profile, what he gave with one hand, Jack took back with the other. In his liner notes, a defiantly underground Jack wrote, "No suit from LA or New York is going to fly to Detroit and check out a band and hand out business cards." Little did he know, but within a very short while indeed, that is exactly what would be happening…

After the *Sympathetic Sounds* album came out and without pausing for breath, Jack and Meg headed to Easley-McCain Recording Studios in Memphis to record their third album. This 'album-a-year' schedule of theirs was so unusual in the modern record industry – even though most bands managed to avoid the five year sabbaticals of The Stone Roses (and an even longer one by the Stereo MCs), most acts with record deals generally spent eighteen months promoting an album before the next record was ready. Not so The White Stripes. They would use up a mere thirteen months from the release of *De Stijl* to the launch of their third long player.

Although some reports have studio owner Doug Easley as producer, the album credits Jack with that role. Stewart Sikes, the sound engineer who mixed that album with Jack had this to say to Brian McCollum about the sessions for this record - which would it turned out, transform The White Stripes from a successful Detroit band into a headlining global act. "We just set up and they started going. Jack knew what he wanted. Meg didn't really think they should be recording - she thought the songs were too new. She sort of drank a few bourbons and smoked a lot of cigarettes. I think Meg was a little nervous being in a big studio, bigger than what they were used to. The main thing I tried to do was make them comfortable so they could play well - with Meg, making sure her part didn't totally suck. She was pretty self-conscious about it."

He continues: "They came for three days and did most of the songs, then came back for two days and then we mixed the thing the next day. Jack told me more than once not to make it sound too good. I knew what he was talking about - from recording at their house to a twenty-four-track studio. We didn't come close to using all those tracks. Basically he wanted it as raw as possible, but better than if it was recorded in somebody's living room. He steered me that way, and I ran with it." Memphis had been an inspired choice for the third album sessions and once again the cost was miniscule – reports suggested the mix was completed for between $4,000 and $6,000, depending upon which reports you read.

Even with the breath-taking debut album widely available from independent record stores in the UK, there were still those who thought The White Stripes were a gimmick, a stunt, a band based more around novelty ideas and costumes than music of any worth. To be fair, without listening to their records, they do indeed have all the traits of a classic novelty act.

Such preconceptions might frustrate most bands but not the Stripes. "That's great for us because it weeds out anyone who doesn't want to dig deeper," Jack told *Kerrang!* magazine's Ian Winwood. "It's like, if that's what you think then great, go away. It was a great litmus test."

Nonetheless, for many, the White Stripes were just a strangely attired two-piece with limited appeal from a city that was famous for making motor cars. Their third album, entitled *White Blood Cells*, changed all that.

The album opens with the informal clatterings of what sounds like Meg setting up behind the drum kit. The first track, future single 'Dead Leaves And The Dirty Ground,' references The Doors track 'Five To One', with an uncompromising shatter of guitar riffs. The duo are very tight on this album opener - as usual Meg's drumming is uncomplicated, kicks on every second beat and leaves plenty of space for her partner's vocals and guitar. Setting the pace and the mood of the album, this is a slower, darker song than one might have expected after 'You're Pretty Good Looking (For A Girl)' opened the previous package, but it was picked up as 'Single of the Week' by *NME*, the UK leading weekly rock magazine and a publication that would go on to have a huge part in the Stripes future.

Reviewers noted the breadth of influences evident on the album as a whole - the Stones, the Clash, Velvet Underground and Led Zep amongst others. But several also noted astutely that The White Stripes are greater than the sum of their parts: although the influences are evident, none stands out so much as to preclude their own individuality – for example, as some might say [not the author] that the Velvet Underground's shadow hangs too heavily over the Strokes.

The first single to come from the album, *Hotel Yorba*, opens up on acoustic guitar. Reminiscent of the folkie yearnings of Donovan or Dylan, within seconds Jack's voice reminds the listener exactly when and where we are. This is angst-time again. As on 'Little Room,' The Stripes present another plea for escape, the Hotel Yorba (however funky it may sound) symbolic only of vacancy in a world far away from the house up the dirt road of the verse, a world far away from the stresses and pressures of people telling us where to go, where to be and how to behave. But there is more 1960's influence at work in the chorus, which recalls the twice-played-at-Woodstock Country Joe McDonald anthem 'I Feel Like I'm Fixing To Die Rag.' This was one of the most entertaining anti-Vietnam War songs of the Woodstock era, a sing-along song for the Civil Rights generation. Escape from 'the man' - one of the prime concepts of the Woodstock generation - is therefore an appropriate image, with the neat

106

little reference in the nod to Country Joe, for Jack's own song of escape. The hotel of the title is in fact a known local 'economical' rest-house in Detroit.

'I'm Finding It Harder To Be A Gentleman', the third track on the album, is another breathe of fresh air, another reason to hope that rock 'n' roll is still alive and well and sharing with him the childhood home that Jack White had bought from his parents. Although Jack claims that few of his songs are about his life with Meg, he was still dissecting with an entomologist's detail the finer points of relationships between men and women, boys and girls. Part horny protestation, part post-feminist puzzlement, White's lyrical obsession with the inherent dualism of relationships continues here, a pattern split across so much of the band's work and image. Spiteful and nervy, 'I'm Finding It Harder...' is one of the albums high points. It was also the song that earned him the nickname 'Gentleman Jack' – leading to countless interviews about his concerns for the morales of society and simple things such as manners and civility.

'Fell In Love With A Girl' is the fourth track on the album, a furious, caustic, Buzzcocks-chain-saw guitar burst, a little under two minutes of strangled love declaration and the future single that would be a crucial part of the Stripes breakthrough into global success. The lyric returns to the frustrations of love - the little things that complicate relationships that should be simple are pitched in an adrenaline rush of sound complete with inane "ah-aah" backing vocals - everything you could ever expect from The White Stripes.

'Expecting' is lubricated with a little Jimmy Page/Robert Plant engine oil, a harsh two-minute grind sung by Jack in pure punk mode. Meg's drumming drags the pace back perfectly, giving the track a tension reflected in the accusing lyrics. 'Little Room's poetry belongs somewhere between Talking Heads' 'Once In A Lifetime' (" you may find yourself... "), the beat-symbolism of Allen Ginsberg, and the lyrical economy of nineteenth century poet Emily Dickinson. Musically it kicks off with Meg's uncompromising beat on tom and cymbal, and Jack's "da-da'da" vocal improvisations after the nine lines of lyric proper. Clocking in at around fifty seconds, this is a little song with a big message. The band's impending global success meant that, once part of a thriving local music scene in Detroit, they were starting to be placed under pressure to leave all that behind and move from the 'little room' of the song into a 'bigger room' of international adulation, success, and all the guilt/ wonder trips that go with it. It was clear that Jack, in particular, found this a difficult transition - their own personal and musical economy at odds with a new world of major label marketing budgets and increasing touring costs, their appearances at awards ceremonies where they would be presented with more and more awards increasingly uncomfortable.

While the lyrics of 'The Union Forever' express again Jack's distaste for developed industry and all the trappings of big business, the song comprises lines from Orson Wells' classic 1941 movie *Citizen Kane.* Watching the movie, White picked up his guitar to figure out the song 'It Can't Be Love, For There Is No True Love,' and found himself rhyming and laying together other lines of dialogue from the film. Talk of a law suit by Warner Bros was one of the few negative aspects of this remarkable record's release. Yet surely the song would never incur upon the film's income by suggesting that people would not go see it: far more likely that it would be seen by a whole new audience of Stripes fans. Besides, Jack had done much more than take someone else's work - indeed, this track is a great example of how he is able to take elements within the arts outside of music and make something unique out of the subsequent inspiration.

Based upon minor key guitar arpeggios and interspersed with classic Meg crash-and-burn/metronomic time-keeping drums, the song itself is another example of Jack's developed dexterity tas a songwriter, increasingly fuelled by story-telling (ironically, as a movie, *Citizen Kane* remains on of the best stories ever told), melody and rhythm.

'The Same Boy You've Always Known' relaxes the pace of the album for a few bars, but - with Jack's recurring themes of accusation within a relationship and near-morbid self-reproach - this becomes a tense workout. Meg's drums yet again frame the vocals and guitar so that Jack's vocals are clear. Again though, this clarity is confounded by the writer's tendency to take the central core issue out of the song itself, leaving big gaps for the listener to fill in.

Likened to Paul McCartney's song 'Blackbird,' 'We're Going To Be Friends' cuts the album short with its gentle, rustic, acoustic picking. Away from the anger and the angst of earlier tracks, this is another step into childhood for Jack, the lyrics concerning the innocence of a childhood autumn romance surrounded by books and maths and brand new shoes.

In 'Offend In Every Way' there is a similar clarity of vision, but here White's lyrics are darker - despite patience and humility, there is anger, frustration and bitterness heaped into the aggressive riffing and powerful drumming.

'I Think I Can Smell A Rat' is another theatrical performance. This track sounds almost as if it could have featured in one of the better rock-inspired Broadway musicals of the 1980s, with its guitar chords which are too simple and its lyrics repetitive. But as the tempo sneaks up a beat or two, its clear that this is another Jack White song where honesty, respect and childhood are taken apart aggressively. Rather than the idealistic vision of childhood in 'We're Going To Be Friends', here White looks at the kids of the post-grunge generation, confident in their need to know nothing but what they choose to know, (through Jack's somewhat old-fashioned eyes), disrespectful of their elders and ultimately uncivil, causing the singer to spit the words out with venom. In one sense this is a flippant throw-away lyric in a simple song: in another it is a wail of anger and frustration.

Claiming it to be an approximation of the making of aluminium in a factory, the instrumental 'Aluminum' is a screeching blast of distortion, from the initial twisted vocal and Hendrix-at-Woodstock feedback-driven riff, to Meg's own "there-is-no-point-in-finesse" drumming. Of course, this isn't an instrumental - it is simply free from lyrics. And as such it encapsulates much of what Jack and Meg's music is about without the distraction of literal meaning and reference. This is a song about anger, frustration, pain and rage. It's also a song about how far down one can strip the electric blues format and still come up with something meaningful. Two and a quarter minutes in length, the guitar and drums slow down to a plodding tempo towards the end, the vocal loops never varying but the guitar tone getting earthier and earthier, Meg's battering of the cymbals more emphatic. Like an aged King Crimson, it may offend some ears, but it is bloody good stuff.

'I Can't Wait' is up next. Grungey - a passing nod to Nirvana while winking at 'Purple Haze' from across the other side of the room - is a stomping parade of guitar confidence wrapped around an antithetical wail of vulnerability. Boy/girl songs are one area that the Stripes do best, and in only a few lines Jack encapsulates the frustration and the despair of continuing to deal with a partner after the relationship has gone off the rails.

In 'Now Mary', Jack returns to the pop lyricism of 'You're Pretty Good Looking (For A Girl)', economic with guitar slashes and witty with words, but its faithful dissection of yet another troubled affair leads neatly into the album's penultimate track 'I Can Learn'. Minor chords and gently tapped cymbals develop another frustrated, theatrical performance

109

piece, more sophisticated in its guitar arrangement than elsewhere on the album, typically nailed by Meg's sympathetic percussion.

Album closer 'This Protector' opens up on restrained (but low-tech) piano, sounding like Jack alone on an old church hall piano. The lyrics are initially unclear in the mix and unclear in their meaning. The uncertainty represents perhaps the confusions and lost aspirations of all the characters so far presented on the album. After all that... 'what now?' What other way to wrap the party up but with an admission of confusion? With so much visible and healthy influence, and so much potential, what better than to end on a direction-free note? It could only point the way to something even better next time.

White Blood Cells is a mix of earthy, primitive punk blues and candy-stripe openness. The not-always-successful attempts to broaden the band's sound on previous album *De Stijl* were more successfully achieved here without compromising that initial first flush of enthusiasm evident on *The White Stripes*. Ironic? Derivative? Cynically calculated marketing? The fact is that by *White Blood Cells,* Jack and Meg White had engaged their audience fully and had defined a blues/grunge/punk/garage sound of their own, fully formed and established on every CD player worth its salt.

Over the years, other revisionist bands have taken similar influences, but merely developed a two-dimensional sound inspired by only one line of influence, whereas The White Stripes had a fully formed beast on their hands that could snap and howl or be left to lie quietly by the fire on its own. One minute we're in a Chicago juke joint, the next we're in the playground. One moment they're pulling in the Pixies and Nirvana audience, in another they appeal to the crusty old blues fan. And alongside all of these factions they are developing their own brand new young audience, drawn by both the visual appeal and the new punk ethic of the band. On *White Blood Cells* the White Stripes had come of age.

CHAPTER 11

"A critic is a man that knows the way but can't drive a car."

Kenneth Tyan

The album was dedicated to Loretta Lynn, the first woman in country music to become a millionaire, the singer of sixteen number one country singles, fifteen number one albums and sixty other hits. Born into poverty during the depression of the 1930s, her autobiography *Coal Miner's Daughter* - also the title of her best known song - was made into a hit movie starring Sissy Spacek, who won an Oscar for her role as Lynn. Never compromising her legendary status by crossing over into the pop market, Lynn remains one of the icons of modern country music, a genre which had been so diluted and infiltrated by 'pop' artists in the late 1990s and beyond.

Once again the cover artwork was loaded with symbolism - Jack himself suggests the masked people are bacteria, possibly the media or music fans, while himself and Meg are the white blood cells. He also likes the ambiguity of the word 'sells/cells', and its insinuation of overpowering commercialism. This was the duo's side swipe at the mass of critical attention they had received since *De Stijl*.

The front cover of *White Blood Cells* shows Jack and Meg haunted by a host of black, shadowy and faceless figures, clamouring to touch them with outstretched hands. In a quick double take, the reverse of the inner sleeve shows a second shot of the same scene, the faces of the figures restored, a bunch of photographers and film-makers filming the duo with retro equipment, Jack and Meg happily mugging-up for the cameras. Such is the irony-loaded duality of The White Stripes - one minute brooding with anti-fame sentiment, the next basking in its warming light!

The CD booklet for *White Blood Cells* is the most lavish production yet for the band, a twelve-page affair filled with art images and photos by Pat Pantano, drummer for Detroit bands Rocket 455, the Dirtbombs and Seger Liberation Army, as well as Pittsburgh's Steel Miners. The photographs show images of blood cells, what appears to be a blood-sampling operation on a baby's foot, rich red hair, red and white fabric and - most tellingly (it refers neither to blood, whiteness or redness) the enlarged fingers of blues guitar legend Robert Johnson [Author's Note: Rolling Stone guitarist Keith Richards, upon first hearing Robert Johnson play, is said to have asked "but who's the second guitarist, man?"]. Only a tiny handful of photographs of Johnson are known, this being the most famous, and while Johnson himself beams at the camera, his fingers are incredible: long, sinuous, and with a middle bone impossibly long, snaking around his guitar neck.

The by-now standard paragraph of non-lyric text is the most obscure so far on all the Stripes' sleeves. Again apparently uncredited, it concerns 'eternal truths,' brothers and sisters, guitar slides, neighbourhoods, friendship, the timeless, unchanging duality of north and south, childhood and memory, pride and happiness. It is difficult to ascribe meaning to the paragraph, but many of its concerns are evident throughout the band's songs. Somewhere in this text there are clues to Jack and Meg's fundamental concerns: on the back cover we see them away from the worlds of music, art, marketing and hype, struggling through a rural landscape, Jack helping Meg down an embankment at the edge of water-drenched woodland. Perhaps here is the place really they want to be, co-existent and alone, presaging the quotation on the inner sleeve of their next album: "We shall soon be far away from you..."

Neil Yee, owner of The Gold Dollar, was delighted when Jack and Meg insisted the record release party for *White Blood Cells* was held initially at his venue. "They did three nights. The first night was at my place and then they did two nights at larger venues."

All did not go to plan at first, however. "I almost turned them down for that record release because there was a big argument. They had originally wanted a different weekend - now, my whole thing about running that venue was about doing so honestly, doing everything right and not playing favourites. The White Stripes then needed another weekend but I already had a band booked that night - the Rocket Teens from Atlanta - and I wanted to see them, there were a number of people who had said if they come to town book them - and so I had already booked them. One representative of The White Stripes said, "next time they're going to be too big to play this place" and I said, "You know what, if they can't play with the band I've already booked then I think they already are. I'm not interested." I knew The White Stripes could just do the party somewhere else and we wouldn't have a crowd that night, but the Rocket Teens was a band we wanted to see. If I was only interested in money I would have stayed with my day job, I was doing quite well at that. Eventually The White Stripes said okay but that representative still hates me I think! The band were willing to do it. It was a brilliant show and putting it together was great.

I think it was mainly Detroit people on the scene who came. Oddly enough, I didn't actually know that many people outside of those who came to the venue, because I'd spent years running that place and didn't really get out much. People would say, 'Have you heard of this band?' and I would say, 'You know, if they haven't sent me something in the mail then I probably haven't heard of them.'

For the record launch gig, they played through the entire *White Blood Cells* record in order all the way through. And I taped it. The recording is perfect. I liked them live, but I hadn't really liked their recordings, I actually didn't even pick up *White Blood Cells* until a few months later when the record started getting big."

Meanwhile, out in the big wide world where not everything was red and white, strange and wonderful things had been happening. Rock was back. Or more specifically, retro rock. At the forefront of this latest wave of revivalists were New York's quite brilliant The Strokes. These four painfully stylish musicians formed in the fall of 1998, a year before *The White Stripes* was released. Taking in particular the Velvet Underground as a clear reference point, the Strokes – like Jack and Meg – wrote classic songs with biting guitars and quickly became known for their incendiary live performances.

With their model looks and glossy magazine style, the band were rapidly championed by an excited media, tired of the dull machismo of nu-metal, which would reached its nadir with the awful sterility of Linkin Park. Admittedly, the Strokes drank and smoked and partied hard, they had supermodels for fans, but there was no denying their songs. Their debut album, *Is This It*, was a blinder and although they only possessed fifteen songs, sent the band around the world to huge acclaim and massive sales.

In the wake of the Strokes came a rash of guitar-obsessed bands that also mined older bands, although none so skilfully as the Strokes it has to be said. The media were relieved to have something new to write about and quickly began to offer new tags for this latest 'scene' – the most clumsy of all these monikers was 'neo-garage'. Suffice to say, bands such as the Hives, the Vines, the Datsuns and countless others (many of whose names began with 'the') had indeed started what came to be dubbed 'a new rock revolution'. At least one aspect which seemed to tie most of them together was this use of the word 'the' in their names' (a trend which had happened before many times - Blur were said to have chosen that name deliberately because it had no such word in it; Matt Johnson took the irony to its logical extreme and called his band The The).

In America, eventually the all-important modern-rock radio programmers looking for a post-Limp Bizkit remedy also began to champion the band, but for now, it was an almost entirely UK-driven phenomenon. By the time of the release of *White Blood Cells* then, with the UK in particular going Strokes crazy, the climate for a new record by the White Stripes was extremely favourable.

Jack was aware of this changing climate, as he explained in *Rolling Stone*. "It would be Staind, P.O.D., then us and then Incubus. Half of your brain is going, 'What is going on? Why are we even involved with this? This is pointless.' The other half is full of people going, 'No, this is new, a quote revolution in music unquote, and something is going to change now, because of you guys and the Strokes and the Hives, and music is going to come back to more realism.'"

Elsewhere he justified in more detail what others might see as a somewhat Luddite approach: "We have to go back. The last twenty years have been filled with digital, technological crap that's taken the soul out of music. The technological metronome of the United States is obsessed with progress, so now you have all these gearheads who want to lay down three thousand tracks in their living room. That wasn't the point."

However, before the band could really start to work promoting the new album, something very strange was about to happen. In the UK, where they did not even have a record deal (they were still signed to Sympathy at this point in the USA), weekly music mag *NME* was about to put The White Stripes on its front cover. In so doing, nothing would ever be the same for Jack and Meg White again.

Although music papers are often quick to re-write history to make themselves seem more prophetic than they actually are -*NME* did not initially review the Stone Roses debut album, a record it later lauded as one of the finest ever - in the case of The White Stripes *NME* were actually pivotal in that band's colossal success in 2001. On August 8 of that year, as mentioned, *NME* put the band on their front cover. This was despite their albums only being available on import.

In fact, in many ways to most music lovers The White Stripes were acutely unfashionable at that point. Word-of-mouth was strong and they had a not inconsiderable live following, plus there had been critical acclaim for sure. Yet they'd had barely any 'substantial' (ie. major magazines) US coverage and their most recent album, *De Stijl*, was hardly to be found in the end of year 'Best Albums' lists. Improving and moving upwards for certain; the next big thing? Absolutely not.

Of course, this has often been the beginning of the end for many promising bands, prematurely thrust into a harsh spotlight before they are ready, only to be shot down in disastrous flames when that fact becomes apparent - Menswear being the most famous example. Conversely, when Suede were introduced as 'The Best New Band In Britain' on *Melody Maker*'s front cover, it not only turned out to be a sizeable blessing, but also pre-empted the explosion of British music that evolved a couple of years later into what became known as Britpop. Yet, in their defence, *NME*'s Stevie Chick (who first saw The White Stripes at an independent music jamboree in Austin, Texas) said, "it's the *NME*'s job to blow things out of proportion!"

It wasn't just *NME* readers who were introduced to the duo so dramatically. Somehow, The White Stripes cover feature had a mesmerising effect on the rest of the British media. Within seven days, they had been written about by virtually every publication of note. *The Daily Mirror* even went as far as to vainly try to christen the implied new rock revolution as 'blunk rock', whatever that means. Numerous other magazines and newspapers were falling over themselves to acclaim the duo - including *The Daily Telegraph*, (bizarrely perhaps) *The Sun* and even BBC Radio 4's staunchly 'Middle England' *Today* programme.

Word then got round of John Peel having said that The White Stripes were "as important as Hendrix and the Sex Pistols". He didn't of course, but as a consequence the hype had been ramped up several notches further. The veteran DJ recounted to me how he came to hear the Detroit duo and his subsequent relationship with the band.

"The very first time I became aware of the existence of The White Stripes was when I was in Groningen in the Netherlands for a music festival. There is an excellent record shop there called Plattenwrn, which is the main reason I go to Groningen really - the music festival is always rather tedious so it's going to this shop in Plattenwrn that is the lure. They'd got the first White Stripes LP there. It just looked an interesting record, the artwork was interesting and the song titles were things that resonated with me in some way. So I bought it and brought it back home, listened to it and started playing bits of it on the radio.

For me the great pleasure of doing my programme is in the discovery of stuff that people won't have heard, or might not have heard, and so I can put it on the radio and they can say, "wow that's great". I get more records and tapes coming in to the studio than I could conceivably listen to. I'm not complaining about this and obviously most people would find this almost their dream situation, but because I have a conscience about it, it bothers me.

But then at the same time I also go around record shops every week, whether here or abroad. You can find you can be given something in the street and play it on the radio that night which to me is the great beauty of radio and it always disappoints me that Radio One has this system whereby records are considered for weeks by panels of people before they're put on the air. By doing that they miss the opportunity to be spontaneous and exciting.

The White Stripes vinyl fitted in with that thinking. I had no prior knowledge of them whatsoever but it looked interesting and she's got these terribly strange, white legs. Also it was in Liverpool colours which, as far as I was concerned, gave it an added interest!

I just thought it was a good record and I enjoyed it and I felt that the listeners would as well. [As for saying they would have as much impact as Hendrix and the Sex Pistols], I didn't say that, but of course you say all kinds of mad shit over the years. I can't always remember what I said yesterday...

The point was I found that record out at a time when music was getting a bit kind of solid and reliable. I always like anything that refers back, you know, to classic R&B and blues. That's what I used to listen to when I was in Dallas and a very impressionable lad. I used to listen to this 'Kat's Karavan' programme and several other programmes as well, it was all Elmore James and Howlin' Wolf, Muddy Waters and people like that. That was the thread that I picked up in The White Stripes, I guess.

Years later they did a live programme for us at Maida Vale and we went round the corner to our favourite Thai restaurant, myself, Louise Kattenhorn my producer and one or two others. We were talking and The White Stripes were quite interested in what I'd got to say. The sad thing with British bands is it's in the nature of the demands of the audience that they mostly can't acknowledge having heard anything more than a couple of years old, because it makes them seem uncool to the NME's readers. So they'll acknowledge the fact that they've heard the occasional Oasis record but they won't go any further back than that. Whereas with the White Stripes, I mentioned that I'd been at the Gene Vincent and Eddie Cochran concert at the Liverpool Empire three or four days before Eddie Cochran died - later that same night, The White Stripes finished their set quite spontaneously with a Gene Vincent song and an Eddie Cochran song. And I thought let's see Radiohead match that! I was impressed by their attitude and their knowledge. We really liked them. Because they just seemed like fans, not of me, but of music. So all they wanted to do was talk about music.

I think that they're part of a noble tradition and in fact, for me, they're a more interesting band than the MC5 and the Stooges. The MC5 I quite liked when they first started. I was never really into the Stooges, I must admit. I know that people see them as being like a seminal band and so forth but it just never really got to me. In fact, I much preferred Tamla Motown to be honest. There's something in my nature, I don't like theatricality much. You get a lot of bands and you feel they're more kind of theatre than they are Rock. I had a basin full of that in the mid-to-late 1960s, so I just don't want any more of this. That's one of the things I liked about The White Stripes – they just kind of did what they did.

The only comparison you could make with Hendrix was that they too have this sort of sense of making it up as you go along. Which obviously is quite exciting. When you go to the big shows nowadays, the principal front man could die and yet the technology would take over and the show would still continue seamlessly towards conclusion. With The White Stripes, you felt there was the possibility that it might go wrong. And that kind of tension seems to me to be essential really.

I did gigs with Hendrix in 1967 and 1968 and I remember seeing him play and you'd think, "fuck me, he's really gone too far this time, he's going to have to stop and say, 'sorry we're going to have to start this number again.' And then he would suddenly and miraculously bring it all back on path again and you'd just be recovering from that and he'd be off somewhere else. You know that kind of excitement and tension is very rare and you got the same sort of feeling from The White Stripes. I suppose it is brave to be like that."

The White Stripes' first UK gig, at London's famous 100 Club - home to some of the most notorious punk gigs ever - could have been sold out ten times over according to the venue's owner. He was reported in the press as saying he had not seen anything like it since the frantic heyday of Oasis in 1994.

A similarly rammed gig was at the Boston Arms in Tufnell Park, where the rock glitterati in attendance, as well as supermodel and future Stripes video star Kate Moss (just the first of a number of high profile Stripes fans). This gig was the final date of a small UK tour just after the *NME* front cover. With the strong underground word of mouth having now been complemented by overground media coverage, the gig was the hottest ticket of the year and many known record industry faces had to be turned away from the crammed venue. It all suggested that something very big was about to happen.

Yet during this hectic week, most interview requests for the band were turned down, especially radio ones. Many anxious journalists talked to the band's UK distributor at Cargo Records, Simon Keeler, in the vain hope of trying to secure an audience with the duo. It was as if the duo already knew this hype could spiral out of hand and were trying to dampen it - yet this probably just served to fuel the fire. The band could do little about this – they had no manager, no lawyer and no publicist to help out.

Simon at Cargo had been finding out such new music for years: "I've always been interested in underground and independent releases from the US, even as far back as the Gories. That was all very exciting and obviously when you hear something like that from an area you always think 'wow'. There were all these great little 45's. Obviously there's the Motown stuff from that way as well, but now there was all the bands with great, fantastic little singles. Sometimes I might only sell less than ten of these singles. No one cared, no one cared.

I didn't like Brit Pop – it was shit. I really went off rock 'n' roll and guitar bands and the fact that Britain had this thing that celebrated itself which was really boring, bland and uninteresting. British music fans were desperate for something new and, although it wasn't completely new, it was bloody exciting and a damn sight more interesting than the bland mass produced crap that was forced upon people over here. It just had a bit more balls."

Simon was not alone in thinking this. This August, 2001 mini-tour and continued praise from Peel mean that the Stripes were the most talked about new band of the moment, alongside The Strokes. "It was an extraordinary time," Peel told journalist Brian McCollum. "The thing was, it wasn't hype. *NME* has a kind of an obligation to find a new sensation every week, because that's what sells the paper. But I think people were just relieved at the simplicity and the directness of The White Stripes, and the fact they were making a noise they could identify with. It was extraordinary that people did take that much of an interest in the White Stripes, and I like to think it was in part because they'd heard the band on the programs I do, and thought, 'Hey, actually this is pretty good!'"

118

Actually, behind the scenes Jack White was furious. He had once called the UK wary of a nation he has called "the most fickle of any place in the world." So he was not best pleased to be an apparent flavour of the moment. "We were really angry," he later told that same magazine. "We asked *NME* not to put us on the cover and they did anyway. We honestly thought it was going to destroy us. We thought the English press was going to chew us up and spit us out and we'd be left holding the bag. To be honest, we just wanted to go home."

But they couldn't go home. They had to stay and face the onslaught and undergo what was effectively a light-speed crash course in media management and career survival. Fortunately, The White Stripes came through relatively unscathed - which is perhaps one of their greatest achievements to date.

CHAPTER 12

"A classic album is something which people praise but don't actually listen to."

Anon.

With such tiny studio costs, *White Blood Cells* must be one of the most profitable albums ever made, a record that would (eventually) become a big hit on both sides of the Atlantic, and an award winner including three MTV Video Music Awards.

The critics continued to be hypnotised: *"White Blood Cells* doesn't veer far from the formula of past White Stripes records; all are tense, sparse and jagged. But it's here that they've finally come into their own, where Jack and Meg White finally seem not only comfortable with the path they've chosen, but practiced, precise and able to convey the deepest sentiment in a single bound," said *Pitchfork* magazine; "Few other performers have electrified country blues to such plaintive and non-parodic effect since the heyday of Led Zeppelin," said *Uncut* while *Q* magazine said it was full of "sonic ingenuity".

Many people talked of *WBC* in the same hushed tones as the first time they listened to the Pixies' remarkable *Surfer Rosa*. Lofty comparisons flooded into XL's press office. The band's web site, run by Ben Blackwell, saw its mailing list increase from the one hundred fans it had been static with for some time, to 21,000, within six months. Within the next twelve months, Jack's publicist was so bombarded with requests that she had no choice but to leave a voicemail saying, "If this is about the White Stripes, I can take requests by e-mail only."

With the significantly greater exposure, it was inevitable that the independent-rock community would battle for the privilege of releasing the group's next album, with everyone from Sub Pop to Kill Rock Stars to the Beastie Boys' Grand Royal label jostling for pole position. Eventually, Richard Branson's V2 won the day in America. Talking to Brian McCollum of *The Detroit Free Press*, V2 President Andy Gershon explained his decision: "I took over V2 in summer of 2001, after being out of the business for almost two years. I asked one of the assistants here to make me a tape of bands she liked, bands she thought V2 should be looking at. So I'm listening to this cassette in the car as I'm driving over the weekend. She'd put on 'Hello Operator'. I thought it was absolutely magical, absolutely brilliant. I went out and got *De Stijl* five minutes later. Then I found the first record, and then *White Blood Cells* a day later. This was the type of band that I found completely fascinating musically and conceptually. I figured this will never get on the radio. But I didn't care about getting hits. I just knew that musically they were doing something fascinating."

The deal wasn't just a straight-forward record contract, but recognised Jack's immersion in the underground music scene over the past years. It allowed Jack his very own label - Thirdman - within the V2 empire.

It got better for the duo too. In the UK, XL Recordings – home to the biggest hard dance band on the planet, the Prodigy – won jack and Meg's signature... for a cool £1 million advance. In both territories, the album was then put out (again in the USA) with the mighty backing of these two major labels. The move up in scale worked - *WBC* eventually passed the million copies sold mark across the world - and in the wake of the band's huge fourth album, that figure would explode once again. The record would go on to gross over $9 million worldwide, a substantial return for their record labels in an era when record companies were notoriously unprofitable. In light of the financial impact this would have on him, when asked if his day-to-day life had changed, he said, "Not really. I still live in the same house I was born in. But I had my chair reupholstered by someone else; I don't do it myself anymore." Despite this coyness, he knew things would never be the same again. "(Previously) we'd been afforded the opportunity to make an album and that meant we didn't have to have day jobs," said Jack in *Kerrang!* "That's what success meant back then."

By contrast, what Meg had not told anybody back in Detroit was that for all this time she had been keeping the uniforms and attire from her old bar and restaurant jobs, just in case the band didn't work out and she might be forced to return to her previous line of work. Not any more. Now, within the space of a few months really, she and Jack had gone from having just enough money to survive (remember that sub they got from Pavement?) to having enough money in the bank to never have to work again... ever.

Neil Yee, owner of The Gold Dollar, has no doubts that the British press (and subsequent public) interest was the catalyst for the band's quantum leap to international stardom: "We all look at it from Detroit as how they hit in England way before they hit here. Of course, a lot of people knew about them here, they were doing well and everyone liked them, but it wasn't that far ahead of anyone else."

It was interesting to see because I really like them but I couldn't figure out why any one else did. A few friends of mine really liked them too, but to me I didn't think it had that mass appeal to it. I knew Jack was really good, of course. I thought he should get somewhere, after all his voice has always been amazing and his guitar playing makes every note count. But this wasn't how I pictured it."

It wasn't just the UK, however, that had been converted to the cause - the USA had fallen in line too, albeit some time later. *White Blood Cells* rocketed past sales of 650,000 in that territory alone, a sizeable achievement for a band who only a few years previously had almost no national following in that country at all. They even played a homecoming show in Detroit itself, to *3,750* fans at the Detroit Institute of Arts in November, 2001.

In a bid to immediately reinforce this new-found high profile, the jaunty single *Hotel Yorba* was released in that month. This was arguably was the first time that the band had genuinely come to the wider attention of the music world, not least from the fact that it was the very first single of theirs to receive a full UK release. This back-to-basics sound is complemented by a cover version of the Loretta Lynn song, 'Rated X', once again showcasing Jack's eclectic record collection. Notably, Jack sings on this recorded version, whereas live Meg tended to take the vocal mike.

The CD also included the video for the track, made by Goober and the Peas leader Dan Miller. In the clip, Jack and Meg are seen sitting on a bed in Hotel Yorba itself, the former strumming on a guitar, the latter drumming on a cardboard box. It is a light-hearted video – even the peculiar shots of Jack with a girlfriend but still tied (literally) by a length of rope to Meg could insinuate all sorts of symbolism but it just seems an interesting but small detail in an otherwise chirpy video. In the UK it reached number 26, a much more lowly position than perhaps their press hype deserved.

A whirlwind tour of Australasia in January 2002, including appearance at the Big Day Out Festival, helped to spread the gospel further round the world. Yet the impact of their next single, the 110 seconds of *Fell In Love With A Girl*, seemed to have the cumulative effect of a million festival headline slots. That release turned what had been great interest in the band in the UK into a full-blown frenzy around them.

Released on February 25, 2002, *Fell In Love With A Girl* was final confirmation, if any was needed, of the Stripes talent. "It has been very organic to this point, but I would say the most calculated thing that they've done was the video for *Fell In Love With A Girl*. Even that they didn't know it was going to explode them like it did," enthused Neil Yee.

The single was the Stripes' most commercial and brutal release to date, possibly their closest to skirting the fringes of the Pixies' sound, accompanied by a now-famous Lego-style video which received much acclaim. In the clip, the band are made from Lego bricks – some actual, some computer-generated and the whole effect was bright, fast and compelling. Consequently, the video found itself on heavy rotation on MTV and similar channels (particularly those whose playlists were voted for by the public) and was the perfect taste of White Stripes after the madness that had surrounded *White Blood Cells* the previous year. It was also the first time the Stripes put out a multi-format CD, with two different CD singles and a seven-inch vinyl – some diehard indie fascist fans bemoaned this as a sign the band were 'selling out' but this of course is elitist nonsense. Old singles 'Let's Shake Hands' and 'Lafayette Blues' surfaced on the various B-sides, as did, oddly enough, the future A-side, 'I Just Don't Know What To Do With Myself'. The final flipside track was a live and truly wild version of Bob Dylan's 'Love Sick' that was recorded during a performance at the London Kentish Town Forum (Jack finally saw Dylan at St. Andrew's Hall in Detroit and maintains this is one of the greatest live shows he has ever seen).

Much has been made of Jack's Dylan fixation but it has been illustrated above that this seminal singer-songwriter is actually just one of many diverse and inspiring artists that Jack likes to draw ideas from. Nonetheless, the fact that this track is from a 1997 Dylan album, rather than the more obvious 1960s epics, suggests that Jack is indeed something of a committed fan. *Fell In Love With A Girl* hit number 21 in the UK charts.

Almost as if to remind themselves of their roots, the day after this single was released, the band played a gig at the tiny venue called 93 Feet East, in London. They were deliberately going back to a 'little room' as Jack once wrote and they were utterly in their element. The lucky few who were there got to see one of their greatest ever shows. After that gig, The White Stripes headed off to Holland, France and Germany for yet more dates, before returning to the US to continue their tour there. Financially secure they may be, but they were not about to retire to a rock star mansion, batten down the hatches and tour once every five years.

While the band was on the road touring this record, somewhat detached from all the furore, one incident served to remind them that the momentum gathering around The White Stripes was escalating exponentially. Word got through to them about an internet sale of an original copy of the first pressing for 'Let's Shake Hands'. Bearing in mind this was a record that had taken years to sell those initial 1000 copies - they were now informed that a record collector had just paid $100 for a single copy. Ben Blackwell was with Jack when he was told the news. "He simply said, 'Oh my God, this is crazy.'"

The huge success of *White Blood Cells* and the on-going critical frenzy around The White Stripes forced them to review their strategy for the follow-up album. Initially intended for a snappy release not long after *WBC*, the sheer momentum of that third record meant the band postponed any successor until yet more exhausting tour dates had been fulfilled. These included European and north American shows in the spring of 2002, most of which were supported by the band's friend and former LA, but born-again Detroiter, Brendan Benson, plus occasional appearances by the Soledad Brothers, the Datsuns, Kid Congo and Pink Monkey Birds. Even now, some magazines were still fuelling the mythology around the band, with *The Independent* calling them, "the greatest brother and sister act combo since the Carpenters."

Although this delayed approach went against everything the White Stripes had stood for in the past, their success had now propelled them into a much bigger league and with that came certain restrictions and conditions. No longer would they be able to press 1,000 copies of a single, sell those on the road and use the money to record a new single. Those were simply cherished days consigned to the crumpled pages of Jack's diary.

To further fan the flames in the insane, whirlwind year that 2002 had become, the band's first two albums were re-released with an accompanying media campaign which raised the hype even further. It was an unsettling time for the duo. "With everything that happened with that album, things became more complicated. I understand *why* they become more complicated, but it wasn't something we were used to." Typically low-key in their response to what is the stuff of dreams for most bands, they seemed acutely aware of the poisoned chalice that such sudden global success could be. Concerned most of all that their burgeoning achievements might ultimately corrupt what they saw as very honest motivations for being in The White Stripes, both Jack and Meg intimated in interviews at this time that there might only be a couple of more albums from them after *WBC*.

Fortunately, there were more singles with almost immediate effect. Next up from *WBC* was possibly their finest single to date, *Dead Leaves And The Dirty Ground*, which would be the last single from that watershed third album. The A-side was a classic, the third in a line of singles that separated the Stripes from legions of rival bands in their quality and variety. Again echoes of Zeppelin but above all an increasing sense of *sounding like The White Stripes,* rather than the countless historical reference points that reviewers were at pains to highlight (necessarily so perhaps). The late and lamented Steve Lamacq's *Evening Session* provided two live B-sides in the form of 'Suzy Lee' and 'Stop Breaking Down', the first a scintillating original, the latter a Robert Johnson cover smashed through a blender and wrenched into the new century. (Note: *Dead Leaves And The Dirty Ground* was not released in the US, just on example of the varied territory/release schedules the The White Stripes use).

The accompanying video was by Michel Gondry, who had also worked with Bjork and Radiohead – it was a White Stripes classic. One obvious influence, on Jack in particular, was Stanley Kubrick's infamous film, *A Clockwork Orange* - most apparent on the spookily addictive video for this single. In the clip, Jack returns from work to find his home has been trashed by a crowd of uninvited party animals, who forced their way past Meg and destroy the house. It is an interesting video with ghostly overlays of both Meg and Jack capturing the initial events and the subsequent reaction, but it is most intriguing for Jack's choice of attire.

In 1971, Stanley Kubrick's highly controversial movie was released to both underground acclaim and mainstream outrage. Based on the Anthony Burgess book of the same name, the film centred around the character of Alex Delarge (played by Malcolm McDowell), a gang leader whose violent life leads to a prison term, which he is released from on condition he undergoes a 'cure for criminals.' This involves mind-altering drugs which create nausea and illness if the subject thinks of sex or violence and anti-social behaviour. This invasion of his civil liberties, set against the backdrop of his gang's own dark, depraved activities, created a compelling paradox. The inclusion of the film's own vocabulary - the gang members were called 'droogs', the language itself named 'nadsat', being half-cockney, half-Russian - added to its allure, as did the affront caused by the 'ultra-violence', namely graphic acts of barbarity, including sexual attacks. This hard edge, the brutal subtext and the highly stylised art direction gave *A Clockwork Orange* all the trappings of a cult classic.

When the film was withdrawn from circulation after a sixty-one week run (rumours suggested death threats to Kubrick's family led to this decision), its status as a taboo yet acclaimed masterpiece was assured. In the immediate aftermath, some youths started wearing the distinctive white outfits, black bowler hats and clumpy boots, a hybrid of city gent style and bootboy intimidation. Others perpetrated copycat acts of violence, which a headline hungry media instantly labelled 'clockwork crimes.' The banning of the film meant poor quality pirate videos quickly started to spring up in backstreets, only adding to its appeal.

For this video, Jack wore the bowler hat and black, sharp-fringed hair donned by Delarge and many others in *A Clockwork Orange*. The look suited him and it became a style that he would be seen adopting regularly at many music industry awards in the coming months. Yet the White Stripes are by no means the firsts band to siphon elements of the film into their own imagery. A crossover with musical subcultures existed as always, with several earlier bands drawing directly on the film. Major Accident, the Violators, Blitz and the Clockwork Soldiers all openly admired Kubrick's work, whilst California's Durango 95 took their name from the car driven by the droogs. The Adicts were perhaps the biggest fans, with lead singer Monkey dressing up entirely as a Clockwork skin and aping Alex Delarge's disconcerting grin to perfection. Their album artwork also depicted scenes from the film.

The year 2002 was also notable for a series of hugely popular and intensely reviewed collaborations at live shows. In the most simple form, these included cameo appearances with Beck and joining his namesake Jeff Beck on stage to play a collection of Yardbirds songs at London's Royal Festival Hall in September 2002. Another peculiar pair of shows was two October dates supporting the Rolling Stones at the Toronto Air Canada Center and the Columbus Nationwide Arena. Unlike when the Strokes did the same, the Stones were interested enough to watch the entire Stripes show from the side of stage.

Then, in October they played a free show for 9,000 people in New York's Union Square. The gig was notable perhaps mostly because it was sponsored by car giant Nissan. The duo had thought long and hard before agreeing to the corporate-backed show, and ultimately felt the ability to offer so many fans a one-off free show outweighed their reservations. Even when the gig was announced and before it was actually played, this motivation was lost in a flood of negative press. Jack ruminated on the barrage of criticism this decision poured on the band and had this to

126

say in *NME*: "Each situation has its boundaries. We're offered so many stupid things - music for video games, horrible films that want one of our songs, beer ads, stupid festivals that want to lump us in with bands we want nothing to do with. We have to constantly turn people down and sometimes it gets to a point where you think, 'This is insane. I can't believe we are turning down millions of dollars all the time.' It starts to sicken you after a while."

In his defence, Jack said "how many people today remember that The Who made a stupid Coca-Cola commercial in the 1960s? Nobody remembers at all. All they remember is the music, that will be kept alive."

Then, when they stepped in at the last minute as a replacement for rapper Nelly on the famous *Saturday Night Live* TV show, the band were again lambasted for not pulling out of the appearance once they found out that the guest compere would be right-wing Republican and Vietnam veteran, Senator John McCain - a man who had publicly berated Eminem for what he saw as a negative influence on youth.

Such criticism is a cliché. Bands have been accepting the corporate buck for decades and those with verve and genuine talent are able to do so without it affecting their material and muse one iota. The 'credibility' that so many fans decry as having been lost is ludicrous – taken to its logical extreme, if a band 'sells out' by playing a big gig or signing to a major who will sell millions of records, then are the same band's only genuine fans the actual people who started the group in the first place? Or maybe the six people who were at their first gig?

Admittedly, your gig being backed by a global car giant is hardly the same as playing for free to raise awareness of 'Make Fair Trade' (as Coldplay do) or some other charity for example, but the alternative for the band was to either not play the show at all ("The White Stripes don't gig like they used to, they are getting complacent") or charge fans for the privilege ("It's not the same anymore, I remember the day when you could watch them in front of fifty people, buy a T-shirt and still have change for a kebab etc etc").

Jack gave such snobbery short shrift. "We didn't want to play to the same fifty people for ten years. Some people claim they have a secret band and react badly when more fans get to know of us. Yet, some of these people only heard of us via *White Blood Cells*, but they are still saying we have sold out! I just think, 'But you've only just got here!'"

Perhaps the Stripes most notable shows of 2002 were in August with the other media darlings of the moment, The Strokes, in New York and Detroit (at Detroit's Chene Park, New York's Irving Plaza and Radio City Music Hall respectively). Chene Park was a 6,000 capacity outdoor amphitheatre - a real sign of the band's arrival back in the States as a major act. The highlight of these extraordinary gigs was when Jack joined The Strokes on stage to blast out the guitar solo for the latter's 'New York City Cops' at the historic Radio City Music Hall. Julian Casablancas was still on crutches after breaking his foot so the whole show made for quite a spectacle. Add to that the scenes of chaos as the two bands chatted to several hundred fans from their second floor dressing rooms - Meg chatted with male admirers from a window, Jack caused a scrum when he threw one of his red T-shirts into the crowd while Strokes drummer Fabrizio Moretti pretended he was going to leap out of the window altogether. One fan quoted in *NME* said, "it was like Sinatra hanging out of his dressing room windows at the... Paramount theatre in the 1940's." Only the lack of a rumoured appearance on stage by Beck (who was in the crowd) came as a disappointment. Otherwise, this was the two biggest new rock bands of the moment mesmerising the crowd and the watching world.

On the surface Jack said they agreed to these dates because "we wanted to show there's no competition or rivalry between us and that we're friends. We didn't want it to turn into some stupid Blur Vs Oasis thing" (there was also some talk of eventually recording a split single together). Behind the scenes, however, the two bands shared much in common, not least a recent and meteoric rise to fame.

The two bands had been increasingly intertwined, both actually and in the eyes of an excitable music press. On these aforementioned joint tour dates, the critical acclaim for each night's show was rabid. Naturally, when The Strokes were confirmed as playing the Reading/Leeds festival in late August of that year, many Stripes fans were desperately hoping for a cameo appearance from Jack. And that is exactly what they got. As the Big Apple rockers launched into 'New York City Cops', on strode Jack in full red regalia (what else?) to join in on guitar. Cue 60,000 festival followers going berserk. Afterwards the media announced this was "the greatest gig the Strokes have ever played on UK soil." Maybe Jack White should think about a more permanent role in their band!

Of course, The White Stripes had played themselves at a hard-to-believe daytime slot of 4.25pm, *earlier* than pop bastards Daphne and

Celeste had appeared two years previous for the ill-received set amidst a shower of piss bottles. Yet somehow this made the performance all the more special, knowing that it should have been the headline act. With this festival's rich heritage, lofty comparisons were bound to spew out after the Stripes raucous set, the most complimentary one perhaps being the analogy from a mesmerised *NME* that "Dolly Parton's kitsch calling card' Jolene' resembles nothing less than 'Smells Like Teen Spirit' in a Stetson. Perfect." This show was complemented by another breath-taking performance at that year's Glastonbury.

Two more Detroit shows - at the Royal Oak Music Theater, Chene Park and Clutch Cargo's cemented their position as the city's most high profile rock band. The city had already acknowledged their success when the Stripes won two Detroit Music Awards, including 'Outstanding National Album' and 'Outstanding National Single' at the twelfth annual event in April 2002.

The year ended with Jack being voted the 'Most Cool Person On The Planet' by readers of *NME*, with Meg at Number six. Not bad for a slightly geeky schoolboy with few friends and a fixation for blues guitarists that no one had ever heard of.

CHAPTER 13

"What the hell is it good for?"

One myopic engineer's reaction to an explanation of the micro-processor.

Things are never simple with The White Stripes. That is what makes them so fascinating. Just when you might think that the years of gigging and playing to handfuls of people were a dim and unpleasant memory, Jack revealed that at times he craved the intimacy and simplicity of his former days in Detroit. Industry insiders were talking of a growing unease within the White Stripes' camp.

The most acute and public example of this discomfort came when Jack and Meg were invited to the 2002 MTV Movie Awards, the latest in a string of increasingly high profile ceremonies and music industry bashes they were being invited to. This wall all perfectly normal and to be expected of course, given their massive profile of late. However, Jack was particularly uncomfortable as he roamed around the Shrine Auditorium in Los Angeles. "I can't even fathom why they asked us to perform here," said the bemused guitarist to journalist Neil Strauss who was reporting the event with them that night.

They bumped into party hard rocker, Andrew WK, who told them he wasn't from Detroit proper; they watched in bemusement as Kelly Osbourne baited Eminem and his bodyguards in a back-stage corridor; but worst of all, they were forced to walk down a particularly lush red carpet while a booming compere announced their band names to a fawning crowd of on-lookers squeezed up against metal barriers, as if the duo were just about to fight Mike Tyson in Las Vegas. Jack and Meg were visibly mortified and scurried down the walk of fame, avoiding all interview requests before they headed inside.

So before they even got to the stage, they were in a daze (Meg tried to combat her nerves with some press-ups - she managed two. "I can do more.") "We've never aspired to this level of attention," Jack said to Strauss before going out onstage. "Look at all the money they spent. This is ridiculous. I don't know why we're doing this." Notably, this last quote solicited a raft of criticism from both media observers and fans who accused Jack of being an ungrateful bed-sit poet - if you don't like the heat etc - but to be fair he was simply pointing out the absurdity of a back-to-basics blues duo being in the same company as acts like Justin Timberlake et al.

Jack is also uncomfortable signing autographs - not least given the statistic that 95% of such scribblings are lost within a week of being given. However, he initially tried to avoid giving them but soon gave in, probably recognising the potential for bad publicity and the realisation that "sometimes you just have to give the people what they want." He was learning, and fast.

This wasn't the only negativity around the band during this time. There was, perhaps inevitably, a cloud on their horizon at the end of 2002, namely a festering feud with Ryan Adams. Initially, Adams was a staunch supporter of the duo, writing a lengthy and hugely flattering biography of them on the web, telling the press that they made him want to "eat crack pipes and dance with the voodoo bones of the dead." He went into minute detail about his emotions on seeing the band play live and just how that had reignited his passion for music, later stating that the Stripes' recent album was "the greatest ever". He even started covering Stripes' songs in his set, inventively altering lyrics to his own particular twist.

Unfortunately, this is where the two musicians seem to have agreed to disagree. It was reported that Jack left a posting on his own web site criticising the way Adams was changing Stripes songs. This infuriated Adams. He subsequently derided the Stripes singer as "little girl Jack" and later called them both "badgers". The White Stripes, eager not to find themselves in some kind of press feud, became reluctant to answer questions about the matter if at all possible, suggesting it had perhaps been blown out of proportion somewhat.

This was not the only sign of other artists playing Stripes songs. There was already a hybrid UK covers act called the White Strokes, internet rumours of a Casio-led easy-listening tribute act too and, perhaps best of all, there were MP3 files available on the internet which had been spliced with the missing bass guitar lines. The man behind this ironic and witty tribute to Jack's songs was Steve McDonald - better known for his years with hardcore-power-pop act Redd Kross. Without approaching the duo, McDonald recorded the bass parts and even superimposed himself - clad in red and white togs of course - next to Jack and Meg on the cover of White Blood Cells, suitably rechristened *Redd Blood Cells* for the occasion. When Steve met Jack backstage later in LA, the latter enthusiastically gave him his blessing!

The final taste of the bands for the year 2002 came as a festive gift to their by-now enormous fan base, with 'Merry Christmas From The White Stripes'. Although this had little in common with the dozens of saccharine yuletide songs that filled every shopping mall in every city across the Western world, it was a fun way to sign off what had been a monumental twelve months. An instant collector's item, the A-side track, 'Candy Cane Children' - a term Jack had taken to referring to Stripes fan by - bemoans the pitfalls of love, with not a slither of festive spirit in sight. This track had actually first surfaced on a compilation in 1998 on the aforementioned Flying Bomb Records. B-sides were a wobbly version of 'Silent Night' by Meg and a spoken word piece, 'The Story Of The Magi' by Jack, making it hard to resist the temptation to ask if he was dressed as a (red) Santa Claus in the studio.

Jack was keen to play down the hugely successful year and remained modest about what lay head. "We're sure to disappoint with the next album," he told the bemused press, although he would later claim that this was a deliberate attempt to dampen what he saw was unrealistic expectations for their fourth studio record.

This next album, to be called *Elephant*, has a somewhat anachronistic tale behind it. Although it would eventually released in April, 2003, it was recorded a full year earlier, while the band were in the midst of the full press on-slaught over *White Blood Cells*. The White Stripes had continued their lightning fast schedule of recording full length records but, finally, their expediency was defeated by events overtaking them.

Much has been made of The White Stripes choice of studio to record this highly-anticipated fourth album. Jack's much-discussed search for purity and 'honesty' in his music led him to root out a studio that did not threaten to suffocate him with zeros and ones. Hence he found himself walking down that dingy alley and under the plastic entrance roof and into Toe Rag, a low profile set up just off the Lea Bridge Road in Homerton, near Hackney, north London, one of the country's poorest boroughs. The studio itself is located down a narrow alley sandwiched between two semi-detached houses. Abbey Road Studios this was not.

Liam Watson, who owns Toe Rag, first met the Stripes when his own band, the soft garage rockers the Masonics, supported them at an earlier UK show. He was known to dislike drug use in a studio and preferred to work cold sober, which fitted neatly with the Stripes own abstinence.

This was hardly a state-of-the-art complex (although rumours that a swearbox was used to encourage staff to refrain from saying 'computer' should be taken with a pinch of salt). More like a few tiny rooms with an eccentric collection of gear crammed into every corner. The walls were covered with the perforated wooden panels to help with acoustics found in a thousand studios across the world, the occasional one being nicotine-stained and scuffed. The black and white squared vinyl floor added to the overall ambience of minimalism born of budget rather than of choice.

Which is exactly why Liam Watson has created such a unique and powerful studio. Not for him the multi-channel computer wizardry of Pro Tools and digital behemoths (not that such technological advances have, in the author's opinion, had any detrimental effect on recording whatsoever - far from it). Neither does he chase a retrospective approach for the sake of it. After all, the misguided school of recording that insists on using the exact same valve amplifier that the Beatles used in 1966 is forgetting the very fact that had the Beatles been a new band today, they would have undoubtedly embraced every new piece of technology with fervour.

Already it seems the growing mythology surrounding the White Stripes has been applied to these sessions. Much focus has been put on Toe Rag only having equipment pre-1963 (because that was the first big year for the Beatles) and how this perfectly reflected Jack's retro approach and his back-to-basics ethics. Not so. The majority of the gear is actually from the 1980s – arguably a period in time which the Stripes portray very little obvious influence from - and even then has been subjected to ingenious customisation by Watson himself. That said, early speculation that the album's vocals would consequently be filtered through vocoders proved to be just that.

Completed for less than £5000 according to some sources, it nonetheless took three times as long to record as *White Blood Cells*. Normally, a tripling of recording time would be a very serious concern for most bands, but when that only equates to just under ten days in total, it was hardly going to make the band's record company run for cover. This brief stint included writing one third of the tracks at the studio itself and mixing the entire record down too. The mix reputedly took exactly one day.

Specific tracks that were captured so rapidly include the semi-novelty 'It's True That We Love One Another' which was completed in just two hours. As Watson told *NME*, "We recorded it a few months before the other stuff on the album... we were all sat around and just did it live, and then added some piano and percussion after. It was mixed in about twenty minutes." One track which took longer was 'There's No Home For You Here' which Jack sang harmonies on fifteen times, thus creating the Queen-esque backing vocals.

Toe Rag saw thirteen of the fourteen album tracks recorded. Meg was delighted with the approach, not so much lo-fi - after all some of the finest produced albums of all time are products of 1980s technology - but certainly a clarion call to simpler studio work. "We're proud we managed to ignore the outside world," says Meg of this record. We just did it."

They felt this record was more relaxed than *WBC* and they were glad the limitations on that previous album had been widened a little. This time their parameters were to record in another country, complete everything within ten days and only work on an eight-track. The end product, although one which would grace the upper echelons of the world's charts, was still by their own admission "one hundred miles away from popular production."

Although a full twelve months away from release, the record that Watson and The White Stripes captured at Toe Rag was an absolute blinder. This is a harder album than previously, leaving behind some of the idealism of the first three, heavy with heart and mind. Raw, *Elephant* never loses its pop soul - among the Son House and Robert Johnson-isms there are still sprinkles of T Rex and Buzzcocks thrown in. Jack spoke of his interest in 'childishness' in future publicity for the album's release - how young children don't lie, they don't worry about what other people think, care about their appearance or allow their world view to be corrupted.

It was clear that The White Stripes had these issues on their mind when compiling this fourth album. With bass lines courtesy of electronic moulding of Jack's guitar sound, the album's opener is one of the duo's strongest songs yet. Future single 'Seven Nation Army' is another fabulous song from a compositional point of view, a step away from blues yet maintaining the music's spirit in lyric and attack. Jack's distorted vocals over Meg's cut-the-crap drumming is soulful and pained - his slide guitar yelling for help as the vocals look for escape from the 'opera.' Blues images are here plentyful - standing before The Lord, bleeding (emotionally or physically perhaps?), the hounds of hell, hard physical labour as penance/escape, going home - all images found throughout the blues canon. But again there is anger in Jack's attack - this really doesn't sound like a band faking image for image's sake, this is a band with a real vengeance to wreak, a savagery in the guitar and a fuck-you drummer who really are going to take no prisoners if the album continues in this mould.

'Black Math,' the second cut and also a future single, certainly takes no prisoners - another vengeful, raucous, contained explosion. Jack's vocals teeter on the edge of a Marc Bolan impression, and there's much to boogie about in the twin guitar attack. Like 'Girl, You Have No Faith In Medicines,' the album's penultimate track, the roots of this song lie in the deep, growling urban complaint of Lightnin' Hopkins, who - like John Lee Hooker - wrote the book on electric blues guitar.

A chorus of multi-tracked vocals *à la* Queen, rootsy electric piano and rock-hard guitar lines make 'There's No Home For You Here' a flame-thrower song that teeters on the brink of anarchy in its chorus, but which is pulled back to quiet cymbal and gentle guitar for the verse. Around two minutes into the song the guitarist goes completely mad with feedback, squeezes some screams from the top of the fretboard, and after the strangled-choir backing vocals proclaim that there is no hope, the song takes cover in a brief lyrical reference to John Lennon's 'Gimme Some Truth.'

The one track not recorded at Toe Rag, 'I Just Don't Know What To Do With Myself' was recorded at the BBC studios in Maida Vale. In the same way that the old blues men and women would happily play pop songs and music hall ditties as part of their act, so the Stripes tackle one of the 1960s' most beautiful MOR/soul classics, a Bacharach and David song that they make all their own. Since the early 1990s, the continued revisionism of the music scene has meant that nearly every musical movement of the last century has been up for grabs by bands and singers worldwide. The kitsch re-invention of 'easy-listening' - helped by the popularity of the Austin Powers series of movies and started, some might say, by the Mike Flowers Pops rendition of Oasis' Wonderwall' - nevertheless brought to the attention of a new generation of musos just how great some of the songs and songwriters of the period were. Burt Bacharach and Hal David stand tall amongst the best of 1960s hit-makers, and were hip again due to Bacharach's current project with Elvis Costello. Dusty Springfield's standard version of the song is a beautifully smoky, languorous and yearning piece - here Jack and Meg retain that yearning, but mix it up with an angular punk/grunge frustration. The histrionic vocals are reminiscent of Billy Mackenzie of Scotland's 1980s pop phenomenon the Associates, and for each verse the raucous slashing of guitar and drums are brought down to quiet, muted guitar arpeggios hung on sharp on-the-beat kicks from Meg. A major highlight of the album (the Carpenters sing the Clash?), Jack's increasingly manic licks match his resplendent vocals. This cover adds to the range of songs on the album immensely, and White himself called it "the best recording of a cover song we've ever done."

On 'In The Cold, Cold, Night' Meg sings. It's a quiet track, and she sings well although with a fragile confidence. Nonetheless, her voice is clear, bears little affectation, and hits the point home. Her own drumming on the track is almost non-existent, and Jack's softly-repeated riff keeps well clear of her vocal performance again in much the same way that Meg's drumming leaves spaces across all their most successful songs for Jack's voice.

'I Want To Be The Boy To Warm Your Mother's Heart' is a commercially cute song of deep insecurity framed with school-hall piano and rusty bottleneck guitar. This boy's lament to his girlfriend is an open and honest letter of 'how does this work?' love. It has been noted elsewhere how there's a weighty element of childishness - maybe child-likeness - throughout The White Stripes' world, from their physical presence to the simplicity of many of their songs, and here again Jack gets neatly into the heart and soul of a boy who just doesn't know how to get through and into a relationship with this girl. Innocence is the key - although the girl's mother has torn the page containing his number from the phone book, touchingly all he wants to do is "warm her heart." Vocally, Jack starts off sounding like a youthful Rod Stewart and, with the addition of a lyrical piano track, there is even at times a flavour of early Faces songs.

Quiet acoustic picking opens 'You've Got Her In Your Pocket', a gently caustic division observed between a genuinely perfect domestic arrangement (the woman's perception) and one based upon deceit (the man's). If the man's duplicity is found out, what means can he employ to stop his woman from leaving? This may be a yearning, gentle ballad from Jack, but its subject matter is pure Chicago blues.

The most traditional 'blues' on the album, 'Ball And Biscuit' sets off on John Lee Hooker Street for a walk of over seven minutes through dark urban sexual motifs that recall classic blues lyrics of subjects such as "seventh sons of seventh sons". Never forget that for every blues man telling you of his sorrow, there are two telling you how they scored with last night's girl. The lyrical simplicity reflects the ball-breaking egotism and sexual candidness of many bluesmen from the 1930s through the

1960s, and Jack's vocal performance includes little vocal asides that run through John Lee, Muddy Waters and Hendrix songs - indeed Hendrix's 'Red House' is echoed in the blistering solos that punctuate the quieter verses. 'Ball And Biscuit' demonstrates what any fan who had seen the Stripes play live already knew - Jack is a cracking guitarist, free from over-indulgence but indulgent enough to take every valued note just beyond the comfort zone.

The theme of urban dissolution is evident again in 'The Hardest Button To Button', a domestic tale of childhood jealousy and backyard voodoo, of family values establishing themselves against the odds. Recalling the characters of 'Broken Bricks' from the first White Stripes album, cracks begin to show when people aren't utilised to their full potential, and although the song doesn't spell them out, it is clear that there are problems ahead for the characters of the song.

Such issues are addressed immediately therefore on 'Little Acorns'. A recording of motivational speaker, author and Detroit TV journalist Mort Crim offers 'helpful advice' on how to deal with overwhelming problems and sorrow. So, after a minute of listening intently, Jack leans over to his guitar and crashes out a recriminating song in which the kind of advice typified by the motivational speaker is balanced by a slice of real life. Jack's lyrics are witty and succinct - problems of the heart weigh heavier than those to hand, and are best dealt with by ripping them apart. The text of the lyrics, printed on the inner sleeve of the CD package, wrap around the swirling dress of the dancing Meg White, hand in hand with Jack. The message is clear - dump the motivator and deal with your issues in real life.

'Hypnotise' - with its 'as genuine as love can be' lyric - is high-speed, enjoyable punk of the first order, stopping and starting, staggering down chord descensions, rhyming neatly on the beat and stopping dead after one minute and forty six seconds. In the same key, opening with a studio-live grunt of 'yeah' and kicking off with a riff heavy on the Hendrix version of the Troggs' 'Wild Thing,' 'The Air Near My Fingers' is a peon to eternal bored adolescence. Like 'I Want To Be The Boy To Warm Your Mother's Heart,' this is another 'boy-doesn't-know-how-to-deal-with-girl' song, but this time it is the adulation of the singer's own mom that gets in the way of the girl-boy thing rather than the girl's parents. Jack's electric piano - with period touches reminiscent of The Small Faces or Spencer Davis Group - compliments the grungy guitar figures and tense, repeated lyrics, and Meg's drumming has a swinging heavy lilt that mixes up a little post-Nirvana punk.

'Girl, You Have No Faith In Medicine' maintains the fast pace as the album moves towards its close. Back to the sing-along, acoustic feel of *White Blood Cells'* 'Hotel Yorba', 'It's True That We Love One Another' is the fun-packed finish for what is a pretty exhausting album. Meg and Jack rap with former Headcoatee Holly Golightly, Jack dropping his 't's and attempting 'Estuary English' to match his London surroundings is comical, albeit a little dull after the first listen.

Recalling 1950s duets from Dinah Washington and Brook Benton, or 1960s easy listening stars Nancy Sinatra and Lee Hazelwood, Jack and Holly just can't seem to figure out how this love thing works yet again. Meg is on hand to offer yawning snippets such as 'Jack really bugs me,' and a more unlikely way to end the fourth album by The White Stripes would be hard to imagine. To be fair, it is fun, and it's easy to forget how much fun there is elsewhere on this album. Even the musicianship of Jack and Meg - thrashing guitar and tempo-sharp drumming - sounds like enormous fun throughout the whole piece. In the lyrics to 'It's True That We Love…' Jack practices his best avoidance techniques with regard to the subject of love. Meg, on the other hand, is the practical voice of common sense. Does this reflect their roles within the band? … the lyricist running here and there looking for clues and avoiding admitting to his own experience whilst hiding behind a series of myths and fictions, while Meg, foot-stamping on the floor, keeps the band grounded, waiting for Jack's lyrics and guitar solos to come back on board?

This final track, 'It's True That We Love One Another' ends in a very English way - a ripple of applause, a couple of 'jolly good's, and off for a cup of tea" to celebrate. *Elephant* was an album worthy of celebration from start to finish. Easily their best album to date, it suggests that they have a true rock masterpiece yet to come. Like *Hunky Dory* was to Bowie's *Ziggy Stardust*, as *Revolver* was to The Beatles' *Sergeant Pepper*, and as *Nevermind* was to *In Utero*, so *Elephant* may signpost a truly earth-shattering album just around the corner. More than anything, it fulfilled the promise of the band's first album, and built solidly upon the third. And it established The White Stripes as a genuine fighting force for the title of 'best rock 'n' roll band in the world'.

CHAPTER 14

"I've looked up to David Bowie all my life, but now I think he should look up to us."

Ian McCulloch praises his own band, Echo and the Bunnymen.

It would have been odd for most bands to wait almost a year after finishing album sessions for the record to actually be released – for The White Stripes, with their cherished speed of releases, this was agonising. This delay made Jack very uneasy and in the early spring of 2003 during interviews preceding the album's release, he was tangibly unsettled, a discomfort exacerbated by the growing expectations the music industry at large had for the record.

Near-workaholic Jack assuaged this edginess in the only way he knew best – playing live. Unfortunately, even that simple strategy did not go to plan - with a raft of promotional duties lined up to prime the media for the release of their forthcoming new album, the band's seemingly unstoppable momentum suffered a blow when Meg slipped on ice in New York and fell awkwardly, breaking her wrist in two places in the process. The injury needed a cast that obviously curtailed any gigs in the very near future, but more notably forced them to postpone much of this pre-album promotional work.

While recovering, Meg spoke to the media about her increasingly high profile lifestyle and seemed to positively enjoy the celebrities she was meeting. "I met Drew Barrymore in New York and she said she liked the band," she told *The Face*. "That was really cool. I grew up on her. (When we supported the Stones) we chatted to all of them. Mick and Charlie watched us from by the stage, and shook our hands when we came off. Charlie said he enjoyed it. That felt good. You can't ask for more than that as a drummer." Yet her celebrity dream remains unfulfilled: "A guest appearance on *The Simpsons* would be amazing. I wouldn't want to be in a Lisa episode. They're kind of boring. Maybe a Homer one would be better."

Fortunately, Meg's recovery was swift - she lost only six weeks to the break - so they were still able to do the much-anticipated small late spring UK tour. With the band claiming to have never cancelled a gig, the prospect of postponed dates had horrified them both.

One challenge facing the band was that they hadn't actually played the songs that would make up *Elephant* since the previous April when they were recorded. Then, when Meg was given the okay to return to the battlefield, they only had a single week in which to rehearse for the entire tour.

Not that it seemed to matter. Jack found that, perhaps not surprisingly, this UK tour starting in Wolverhampton was their most rabidly received series of dates ever. It was helped by the fact that due to Meg breaking her wrist and live commitments elsewhere in the world, this was The White Stripes' first appearance in the UK since the Reading Festival the previous August. Having publicly expressed a fear that the venues would be filled with Johnny-Come-Lately fashion victims with no real insight or love for the band, Jack was delighted to find that the majority of each crowd seemed to know every lyric of every song, including the older tracks.

Probably the most high profile of these was the double-nighter at Brixton's 4000 capacity Academy, traditionally seen as a step between the medium-sized venues such as Astoria to the arena tours and possibly a precursor to stadium shows. Bands have been broken by one single bad show at Brixton; conversely careers have been made when the south London venue was been conquered.

On the night of the first show, the signs were good for The White Stripes, even before you got inside the venue, where ticket touts were asking for - and getting - £70 a ticket hours before the doors opened. The guest list was rammed, limited to 'plus ones' due to excessive demand. The show had all the signs of being the hottest ticket of 2003.

The *Felix The Cat* cartoon returned again and seemed oddly perfect as it welcomed the excitable crowd, before fading away to allow Meg to saunter on to the stage nervously. Huge applause filled the cavernous room, threatening to crack the famous proscenium arch, only to hitch up another notch when Jack rolled on stage too, walking slowly to his mike - unlike at Wolverhampton a few night's previously when he had crawled to the centre of stage on his belly.

Standing tall in his near-obscene red-and-black-legged trousers, Jack launched without delay into a coruscating version of 'Black Math' and the Academy exploded into mass hysteria. Brixton, London, England, Europe, America, the world was theirs.

Ice T's Bodycount once played the Academy to an audience of almost entirely white kids; equally peculiar was the raucous reception proffered to cover versions as obscure and obtuse as 'Take A Whiff On Me' and Dolly Parton's 'Jolene' (goth ubermeisters Sisters of Mercy once covered the very same). At times it seemed Jack could have tuned his guitar and received an ovation.

Momentary appearances by bizarrely-attired road crew confirmed the suspicion that The White Stripes orbit in their very own sartorial universe. One observer was overheard commenting to *Bang* magazine writer John Doran that "they look like World War Two versions of Run DMC."

That two people alone on stage can make Brixton rock like this was remarkable. That they can do so for two sell-out nights is a triumph. With this quality, they might just skip the arenas and go straight to the stadiums... Ironically, the problem is, can the intimacy and touch that makes their records and smaller live shows so vibrant and compulsive make the leap with them? Jack is not so sure and when pressed on the matter in mid-2002, he suggested such a development might even prematurely finish the band: "We're not going to be around for long. Maybe after this next album comes out, maybe another. We don't have the potential to be an arena-sized act. I don't think a two piece band really would come off in an arena-sized place, it doesn't really have any intimacy." Elsewhere he suggested they would continue to play three or four nighters at smaller venues like Brixton rather than one almighty show at Wembley Arena or similar.

By now The White Stripes live show was staggering. Having waited so long for the album campaign to begin, the pent-up energy and frustration was unleashed in a tidal wave of primal rock. Starting with 'Black Math' on most nights, the gigs were among the very best the Stripes had ever played. "There's something about that song, it's hard to whip out in the middle of a set..." Other than that, however, Jack insists their sets are not worked out in advance and allows ample room for improvisation and spontaneity. Indeed, Meg usually only finds out which songs Jack is playing next at the same time as the audience - he will just strike up a riff or opening phrase and she will just automatically join in.

During the shows, although it seems both Meg and Jack are totally lost in the performance, there is room for nerves. " They are often observed at the side of the stage sucking a last few breaths out of a shared American Spirit filter cigarette - like Butch Cassidy and the Sundance Kid about to face their destiny", as one astute gig reviewer put it.

Jack further explained to *X-Ray* why White Stripes' shows can be so demanding: "I was listening to Tom Jones and thinking, 'Man, he has got it so easy, he really has. He goes out on stage and sings his songs... and his band does all the music.' That feels so easy. He can enjoy it. I can't. I have no time to enjoy anything we do live. There's so much to be done, there's so much propelling of the show and convincing of people, directing what's happening between me and Meg... keeping it rolling. That's all I can think about."

141

There are virtually no stage sets to distract the audience either. The White Stripes are not known for hanging effigies of themselves from the lighting rig or arriving in a fifty foot lemon. With the much more sizeable venues they were playing during 2002-3, they did recognise that sometimes more visual aids might be necessary – for example, on the pre-*Elephant* dates, they screened snippets from the *Felix The Cat* cartoons. Elsewhere, they have draped an American flag as a backdrop, something Ryan Adams has also been known to do.

Their live shows are always a compelling paradox of an apparent struggle/collaboration between Meg and Jack, a struggle within Jack himself and the seamless teamwork that fuses together this innately spontaneous duo's performance. Ever apparent when watching The White Stripes is the unsettling way that your eyes are drawn to *both* Jack and Meg, the former being the maelstrom at the centre of it all while Meg just counter-balances the whirlwind with an almost robotic and hypnotic steadiness – you can almost lose your balance watching those laconic, hypnotic drum strokes.

In post-*White Blood Cells* shows, Jack took to placing a vocal mike in front of Meg's drum kit, so when he screamed his vocals in her direction the clarity was not lost for the audience. A sound engineer's nightmare perhaps, but a nice attention to detail, showing the controlled blend of spontaneity and precision that lies at the very heart of the White Stripes on stage. Although a little abrupt the first time you see it, Jack's habit of simply stopping a song mid-verse if he isn't "feeling" it within a few chords, is an unusual but admirable perfectionism.

Jack's actual guitar playing has been analysed in great detail, a goldmine for the technically-minded. One such aspect of his live performance has intrigued many theoretical guitar experts observers: "There's a technique I have where I can put my pick in the palm of my hand and pluck with my free fingers. And I can pull it out whenever I want to switch it back to the pick to play loud again. It just came naturally, I dunno . . ." He is helped by his (suitably) unique guitars. One is (of course) red and white, another appears to be a cut-away coated with flaking brown paper. Yet another six string he is mysteriously evasive about: "The red one is an Airline, a guitar that Montgomery Ward sold in the 1960s. And the other one is, yeah, it's . . . um . . . Actually, I don't want to talk about that. It's kind of a personal thing."

Due to the stripped down nature of a White Stripes show, the practicalities are fairly unforgiving - if Jack breaks a string, the whole show stops; if Jack is feeling ill - or Meg for that matter - there is no one to fill in while they take a break; they can't even slip off-stage during a solo for a drink and respite, hence they both usually surround themselves with dozens of bottles of water. This is just as well, because the momentum and pace of a White Stripes gig is the musical equivalent of a mini-marathon raced as a sprint. "I hate that dead air. I want it to be, as soon as it's done, '1-2-3-4', let's keep going and exhaust people. If just the two of us can really exhaust people, that really feels good."

Yet conversely, it is this struggle and the show's physical demands that may ultimately be the death knell of the band, simply because it takes too much out of Jack. "I don't know how long I can put up with that," he told *X-Ray*, "how long I can put with not being home, and just draining myself every night. I'm no t taking speed before I go on stage, I'm just using that spoilt-brat mentality, that energy to make something cook up and happen."

The sense that The White Stripes had cooked up something very special with their forthcoming album was reinforced when press samples of the clever and thoughtful artwork for the record were circulated. The images cemented the idea that the aforementioned aspiration to an age of innocence was evident not only in the songs but in the album's packaging. Jack appears clutching a cricket bat, a surreal white stripe against the red background of the photo shoot. Beneath a dangling light fitting, he looks like the wayward ghost of Hank Williams, while a tearful Meg is part country-trash, part Morticia Addams. Dedicated to 'the death of the sweetheart,' Jack spoke of the lack of honesty in modern country music, and if honesty is a form of innocence, then the artwork of the CD sleeve betrays a confusing selection of innocent images more Magritte than Mondrian.

The artwork was photographed by Pat Pantano, drummer with The Dirtbombs and a photographer who has taken shots of many of Detroit's key musicians. The make-up was done by Tracee Miller who is also in a band, called Blanche. The photos were taken at the end of 2002 at a small Detroit studio, soundtracked by a Christmas album of Elvis songs, Jack's choice. The resulting photography shoot led to six different covers, all altered slightly with various poses and outfits for different territories and formats. The artwork was Jack's concept and he styled the shoot too.

Elephant has been described by Jack as the pair's "English album", recorded in the UK, with British references in the lyrics throughout. Jack's cricket bat on the front cover - that weapon of the most English of games - entered Jack's world after DJ John Peel tried to explain how relaxing a day at a cricket match could be. Cups of tea and faux English accents also creep into the mix - a neat return of thanks to the nation who really took The White Stripes to heart.

The media has had a field day interpreting the artwork, referencing concepts such as the death of a lover, a lament on the state of country music, the possible extinction of elephants. The cricket bat, it was suggested, might represent an elephant's tusks, and the silk cord between Jack and Meg is purportedly representative of an elephant's tail – no one seemed to mentioned they are sitting on a trunk (boom boom).

At the risk of fuelling such conceptual speculation, it should be noted there's a little graphic device that crops up on three of the four album sleeves so far (it doesn't appear to be on *The White Stripes*). It's a non-verbal series of three vertical lines, perhaps the Roman numeral III, perhaps a signature (it appears beneath each of the textual elements of the booklet designs as though identifying the authorship of the paragraph). On *White Blood Cells* it also appears on the credits page, as does the western numeral '3,' which is also printed on the side of one of the cameras in the cover art work of that album. The ornate Leslie speaker cabinet on *De Stijl* also includes the numeral '3.' Jack has often said this number is at the core of the band: "This band has always been about limiting ourselves, always been about revolving as many things as we can around the number three. If artists don't make rules, it can ruin why they got involved in music in the first place."

Jack wears button badges with legends such as 'I am 3' on them. "Fire needs oxygen," he told a bemused *X-Ray* magazine, " heat and fuel. You can't have only two of the three components. You have to have all three and no more. Three. It's perfect. Everything I do, I try to revolve it around that number - even our third album was the one that broke us into the mainstream." Wise words indeed form a man fronting an acclaimed... er.. duo.

Some observers mocked such statements as painfully pretentious, others were happy to play along with the ruse. Inevitably, such unexplained touches of detail lead to the 'Paul is Dead' school of rock journalism where 'hidden meanings' are sought that will give the discoverer 'the answer' to everything connected with the artist.

So it is with *Elephant*. The Roman numeral device is on the bottom corner of the amp on which the duo sit for the cover shot, it (once again) authors the lengthy paragraph of prose within the booklet. Reversed, the number '3' makes the letter 'E' on the cover, and is highlighted in red wherever it appears on the sleeve. So what is this all about?

This central tenet of the band goes way beyond *Elephant*. Before the record business, Jack White ran an upholstery business called 'Third Man Upholstery.' The room in his home, formerly his parents' house, where his recording studio is set, is called Third Man Studios. His publishing and record labels are called Third Man. Third Man is responsible for the design of *White Blood Cells*. The colophon-logo of Third Man is a representation of three little men standing in a row - akin to the numeral III.

So now we know the author of the texts within the White Stripes album sleeves - Jack White as The Third Man. Within the booklet for *Elephant* The Third Man rants uncontrollably at the brain-dead culture of (American) youth (and their parents) obsessed with the shallow and the new, divorced from the organic, the historic and the meaningful. This is the death of innocence, the death of honesty, the death of hope and comfort. It is mirrored in Meg's melodramatic handkerchief-to-eye gesture on the cover (is Jack's knock-kneed stare representative of that wasted youth culture, so evidently not heeding Meg's apparent despair?). And, of course, it's mirrored in the music.

Elephant completes a series of albums stunning in their visual impact (the back cover even refers to the three previous albums as 'titles in the series,' as though this were an instalment-based series of part-work publications). Placed together, the consistent themes of red, black and white establish the band immediately for fans and the greater audience of future fans alike (recall John Peel's initial reasons for picking up their record in that Dutch store). Their comic-book simplicity is an easy handle for the youngest pop audience, while their art-school philosophies appeal to the intellectual rock listener. And - countless bands from The Beatles to Bowie, from the Pistols to The Prodigy have shown that having a visual identity that a fan-base can ape is no bad way to inspire record sales either.

Which brings us to the subject of The White Stripes' image. The much-discussed aspect of the band was best seen in a stunning photo shoot for *Q* magazine in their June 2003 issue. Inside there were shots of the duo in all red or all white, surrounded by 1960s and 1970s furniture. Proof positive that their image was evolving, there was also a snapshot of Jack and Meg looking like they had just joined The Strokes, in full black-clad, raven-haired, shades-wearing glory. The best photo was reserved for a red/blood-spattered frame of Jack on his knees, menacingly reaching for the camera lens with Meg perched on a plastic white table (shades of the Stone Roses brilliant debut album cover perhaps, but done with the Stripes very own panache?) *Q* writer Michael Odell accurately likens them in the accompanying piece to "a couple of disgruntled vampires". They were happy to fuel the concept by taking him into the heartland of Victorian-era Jack the Ripper, to view the highly controversial art exhibition 'Body Worlds', containing preserved body parts, anatomical dissections and the like. But don't be fooled - this would not have been a snap decision. Jack White was in total control.

They are certainly an odd couple of rock, in a genre that boasts more than its share of oddities. Meg's teeth are uneven, she claims to collect stuffed toys (Jack disdainfully calls her favourite - a mouse wearing a ribbon - as "comedy taxidermy") and is an expert on junk food from around the world (not that her waistline suggests this). Jack has been known to chain-smoke through interviews, punctuating each long draw on a cigarette with a new pearl of wisdom or to bestow another historical reference point for his music. He then tucks the packet back under his sleeve like some James Dean throwback. Other retro traits include not owning a mobile phone and despising cars (sacrosanct for a native Detroiter).

Much has been made of the fact that The White Stripes on stage are identical to The White Stripes at home, in the street and hanging out with friends. What you see is what you get, apparently. There seems little doubt that Meg is universally liked and admired for her reserved and shy nature – certainly among everyone I have interviewed for this book. Jack, likewise, is praised even by those who have subsequently had disagreements with him, for his aptitude and ability.

Jack's house, as has been described, is like the set of a White Stripes video. He still lives in the same house as before they became famous, but alongside the mountains of furniture are countless stuffed animals, not the cuddly type that Meg prefers but the work of a gaggle of taxidermists. Tiger and zebra heads adorn his walls but perhaps his most prized collectible is an actual two hundred-year-old human skull, which he discovered while rooting around junk shops in Romania during the filming of his first feature film role, *Cold Mountain* (he showed this gruesome memento to co-star Renee Zellwegger and was impressed by her knowledge of skulls and teeth - more of which later). It takes its macabre pride of place on his piano, looking down at him whenever he writes new material. Imaginatively, Jack said of this odd curio that "a hundred years from now, I'd like my skull to be in a junk shop and for someone to pick it up and buy it... but what I'd really like is for the person to wonder, 'Who the hell was he?'" Just imagine the fun you could have with that on e-Bay...

The closely controlled visuals naturally continue on stage too. They have a candy cane drum stool, made for them by artist Paul Frank who also made a red-and-white striped guitar strap for Jack. This complements their swirling red and white drum riser perfectly.

He may have a musical Midas touch, but Jack is prone to the odd fashion disaster, most notably with the red leg/black leg trousers he wore during 2003. He said, surely tongue-in-cheek, that they represented the good (evil) right side of the brain versus the left (good) side dichotomy. He even put a cross on his left hand at one show and was convinced that the show was dull as a result. As for the trousers, however, despite such illuminated reasonings, they make him look less like a candy cane rock icon and more of a pub-singing Liquorice Allsort. Still, even then he was able to entice the sexually preoccupied tabloid *The Daily Sport* to announce that said loons were so revealing as to display he had "the biggest cock in rock". He must be very proud.

Interestingly, despite the frenetic adoration of their millions of fans and the world-renowned image they have, it is not so often that you see a White Stripes fan actually dressed in the same garb as the duo. Usually, when a band reaches such levels of fame, the cities and provinces are filled with clones in varying degrees of similarity, from cool spin-offs to scary *Stars In Their Eyes* look-a-likes. Grunge kids adopted the loser look wholesale and sent sales of Dr Martens boots and lumberjack shirts through the stratosphere. Even Slipknot had their (albeit small) number of fans who had the nerve to go 'up the town' in orange boiler suits, despite the virtual guarantee of a good kicking this secured. This was not a new phenomenon. Rock 'n' roll has for many fans, since its inception, been about image as much as about the music.

Not so The White Stripes fan base. Maybe some male fans shy away from Jack's Dave Lee Roth-tight trousers, fearing for their own future fertility; female fans can occasionally be seen with cropped fringes and white dresses, but generally the band's attire rarely matches that of their audience. This is an unusual trait particularly when it is that very image that helps make the band so popular. It does have to be said, however, that on the April 2003 dates in the UK, with *Elephant* storming the charts, that more look-a-likes could be seen jumping around in the mosh pit. In late August, 2003, the band themselves delved into this growing image duplication by playing a storming rendition of 'Fell In Love With A Girl' at the MTV Award ceremony in New York in front of dozens of Stripes clones. Only the much-hyped kisses between Britney, Madonna and Christina Aguilera topped the Stripes for press coverage.

Jack is clearly the Fat Controller of both his band's image and their music. He unashamedly throws out band commandments into a willing media circle. Meg once said, "If he sees people queueing to buy ice cream, he'll say, 'Why ice cream?'" "Yes!" continued Jack, "how come you see a whole bunch of people buying themselves ice cream? Have they *all* done something especially worthwhile that day?" Of course not, Jack. They just want a bloody ice cream.

Ben Blackwell is keen to dispels the myth that Meg is little more than a puppet for Jack's vision and muse. "As for controlling it all, they both have equal say. A lot of the media make a big thing about Meg never talking, especially in interviews. But it's more that Meg chooses her words very carefully. With some things, she doesn't really have an interest either one way or the other, but if she does have an opinion and feels strongly she will make it known. Her strength lies in her silence. So she does speak up, it's something that Jack will take notice of."

Other 'band rules' include no groupies, no drugs, (ideally) sponsorship or corporate involvement, diva-like behaviour and so on. They smoke because they "started before we made music", but they still don't compile set lists or, supposedly, rehearse. "It's about the truth of things, I always ask, 'Is it necessary? Does it have soul?"

Some of these band commandments seem laughable albeit harmless. Others are to be lauded. Jack is at pains to avoid being perceived as a rock star. People confuse being born as a rock star - like Freddie Mercury - with behaving like an arrogant, self-important brat, like so many divas and rock stars one could mention. Jack himself said during one interview that, "I'd be concerned if anyone met us and didn't get the feeling, 'What a polite young band.'" Jack has earned the nickname Gentleman Jack, like some modern day, guitar-slinging Western cowboy. Sid Vicious must be turning in his grave.

"I do feel I embody values that are out of fashion," Jack told *Q* magazine. "A lot of women just don't go for thoughtful, considerate and kind. I could drink and have sex every night with groupies and really act like an asshole. Sometimes you really hate to see people go out on tour because you don't want them to change. We've really been pretty good people at trying to stay away from that environment... but without wishing to be pretentious, it is very hard for the sweetheart or gentleman to exist nowadays." He goes on to bemoan Ali G-style white kids, parents who don't chastise their offspring for swearing in front of them and teenagers with body piercings.

To those who say Jack is a dullard, he also suggests that the more he abstains the more likely it is that he might fall off the moral bandwagon. So many celebrities have made such a public statement of anti-drug use or similar, only to be photographed snorting an Olympic-sized line of cocaine in some urine-soaked cubicle, prior to said moralistic career imploding amidst public outcry. Whether this fate will befall Jack is up to him and - it has to be said -it is unlikely that such events would in fact dilute the band's popularity. The White Stripes do not sell records because they abstain from the rock 'n' roll lifestyle. It is an interesting and indeed brave standpoint to make in an industry that often rewards excess with sympathy and platinum album sales, but it is not at the core of why The White Stripes are so brilliant. If that was the case, Mary Whitehouse would be receiving a posthumous 'Lifetime Achievement Award from *Kerrang!*

Furthermore, Jack is keen not to be misrepresented as some kind of censorious old woman. As he said to *Q* magazine, "I'm sure you can still have fun and make great music. Look at some of the blues artists or the Stooges... we're not trying to come off as a 'Say no to drugs' band. We don't want to be judgemental." However, such statements will always be used as bullet points to summarise and neatly pigeon-hole The White Stripes. Even in this aforementioned *Q* article, the writer pointed out "you wouldn't want The White Stripes organising your birthday party." Fair point.

Interestingly, Jack has mentioned being envious of Freddie Mercury's rock star mentality - "he loved the monstrosity of being a rock star" - something that Kurt Cobain touched upon in his suicide note. Not that I am suggesting Jack has tendencies similar to those of Mr Cobain, but it is interesting to note just how many rock stars look to Freddie as some kind of iconic and idealistic blueprint.

At times, Jack comes across as pretentious (statements such as "Why wear green for a day, it would be so bourgeois!" don't do him any favours), talking of philosophy, musicology, colours and number theories and such like, but he also seems acutely aware of the absurdity of his position and has a refreshing attitude to criticism in the media: "I love bad reviews," he told *X-Ray*. "Bad reviews don't make me mad. I like to know why they think that... (maybe) they went in and hated us to begin with... or maybe they've got a point." He recognises for instance that they are both a fake band and a very real band at the same time.

Yet there is a core paradox which contradicts Jack's search for honesty within his band – the entire brother/sister myth. If The White Stripes is about the truth of things, then why perpetuate this tale? After all, the actual truth was revealed when, first an internet magazine and then later *Entertainment Weekly* published Jack and Meg's divorce certificate for all to see. Yet, around the release of *Elephant*, Jack would still introduce the band on stage by saying, "I'm Jack White and this is my big sister Meg." Likewise, some magazines still reviewed that album as by a brother/sister duo.

Gary Graff, the aforementioned Detroit journalist suggests this reason for the continuation of this story: "I think they did it for friends at first, just Mr Goof. The fact is that they were married and I think they felt there'd probably be too much attention, too much drama around that and not around the music."

Jack was happy to leave the matter ambiguous, at least in interviews, although he also skirted around it with some of his material. Meg openly sings about being a divorcee on 'Rated X', while on the quirky 'Well It's True... " with Holly Golightly, he is described as a "little brother". However, when pressed on the matter, he just says it was all he could think of to rhyme with "another"!

Whatever the rights and wrongs of this prolonged subterfuge, it is but a small part of The White Stripes grander and utterly fascinating image. Few bands of the modern era can compete with the detail, thought and continuity that the duo have managed to inject into their sartorial presence as well as their artwork. For that they must be applauded. The more important question for The White Stripes in the first half of 2003 was, with *Elephant* about to be released to a highly excited public, would this record be able to match up to the hype?

CHAPTER 15

"I never considered myself the greatest, but I am the best."

Jerry Lee Lewis

As an immediate teaser to the forthcoming new album, The White Stripes released *Seven Nation Army* - surely one of the record's best cuts - as a single in April, 2003. The track sounded as if it had a bass, but this was just Jack's guitar fed through an octave pedal. The anthemic guitar riff and escalating sense of freak-out made this one of the best singles of the year and single-handedly converted thousands to The White Stripes gospel. On the flipside was another nod to their pal Brendan Benson with a vamped-up cover of his 'Good To Me', sitting next to a typically quirky choice of an old American folk song, 'Black Jack Davey which had previously been covered by no less than Bob Dylan and The Gun Club.

The single also inadvertently led to Jack being able to perform with one of his all-time heroines - Loretta Lynn (to whom the previous album had been dedicated as mentioned). The country singer was also Meg's favourite so they were both delighted when she performed with them at their April gig at the Hammerstein Ballroom in New York. Lynn had been in her kitchen at home when 'Seven Nation Army' came on the TV. She later told Jack "it sounds like somebody tryin' to break in to a bank."

That particular show sold out in seven minutes flat (they were later invited to her ranch). Back in Detroit around this time, they played two homecoming shows, first at the Scottish Rite Theater (inside the Masonic Temple), located in the run-down Cass Corridor neighbourhood. At a second larger show at the Temple's main arena. Jack thanked the ranks of Detroit music's inner circles in attendance, saying, "Thank you Detroit, This will always be home, no matter what." After this show, the Stripes continued across north America for yet more sell-out shows before planning to return to Europe in May for more shows. In among this lengthy series of shows was a spell-binding blitz at the excellent Coachella festival in California, putting to shame numerous renowned live acts including Queens of the Stone Age, Beastie Boys and the Red Hot Chili Peppers. Jack sported a black bowler hat for much of the weekend, once more linking the band visually back to *Clockwork Orange*.

For this new album campaign, the duo looked slightly different - longer haircuts and more gothic-tinged outfits - but the essence was very much the same and equally striking. This was perfectly displayed with the accompanying four minute video for the 'Seven Nation Army' single, which was not only a compulsive (if slightly nauseating) clip that instantly found itself on heavy rotation across the growing number of music channels, but was also the definitive example of just how cleverly and strongly branded The White Stripes are. The track had actually been out on US radio for three weeks before they completed the video but this gap did little to dilute its impact.

The simple concept of using red and white is used to extreme here and with great aplomb. As each shot of Meg or Jack encased under a triangular motif zoomed towards the viewer, another clip was already sprouting from within, rather like the infinite images created by two mirrors placed directly opposite one another. Jack had been toying with the idea and was keen to at least have an elephant and the Holy Spirit represented or actually featured in the video. There were even skeletons, courtesy of stop-go animation tricks like those used by legend Ray Harryhausen on classic films such as *Jason And The Argonauts*. There were also said to be references to occult writer Aleister Crowley and Queen's epic single, 'Bohemian Rhapsody'.

It was a hypnotic sequence although certainly not one to watch after a long night drinking... What it did do, apart from promote the single hugely, was reinforce the feeling that here was a band in tight control of their image, a visual signature that was unique in an era when it seemed at times that everything had been done, when many new bands looked like tribute acts - here was The White Stripes proving that new music was as good as it had ever been.

Finally, after waiting for what must have seemed like an eternity, all that was to be done now was prime the media for the new album. Explaining the title of the album on MTV News, Jack said, "There's a lot of reasons for it. One of the main metaphors was that it was one creature that represents both mine and Meg's personality on stage or in real life. It was the two of us in one creature. The notions people have of elephant's personalities being majestic and powerful, but also subtle, innocent, angry and clumsy. It seemed like an animal that represented The White Stripes." Elephants bury their own dead and can remember the burial site fifty years later - even having been observed crying on their return. Thus the White Stripes see themselves.

Yet, even with its release firmly penned in for May, 2003, a problem hit the launch campaign, one that was becoming a growing blight on high profile new albums across the world - the leaking of tracks for downloading on the internet. The record industry's battles with file-swapping sites such as, most notoriously Napster, had brought this issue to the wider public's attention. Despite the relatively successful campaign against Napster, the problem still festered across the web. In the aftermath of that legal battle, file-swapping had gone underground, with individual users proliferating the material and even being chased through the courts for bizarrely huge sums of money (in one instance a twelve-year-old girl was being sued by major record labels).

Elephant suffered a similar fate to many contemporary releases. The first seepage came over two months before the album was due for official release, and within days the record was available to download *in its entirety*. All this despite expensive and extensive security measures put in place by their understandably protective record label XL. They had sent out a very select number of promotional copies - as they have to in order to create a buzz about the record - but *only* on vinyl. Although Jack's own retro stance on many issues was believed to be partly behind this strategy, which in itself was a neat gimmick, it is also a fact that vinyl made it harder for bootleggers to acquire crisp digital copies. These few copies were guarded closely by XL until despatch.

When news of a possible leak reached XL headquarters, the record company very cleverly placed so-called 'spoiler' MP3 files on the web, tagged with genuine track titles but containing only ten-second loops running over the song's entire length.

Eventually all this disappointing dilution of the record's release forced XL's hand into putting the record out a week earlier than originally planned. Arguments continue to rage about the negative effect such piracy may or may not have on actual sales. There are several examples where it appears to have had no effect whatsoever - Eminem protegé 50 Cent brought forward his debut album, *Get Rich Or Die Tryin'*, but still had a million-seller on his hands within eight days. Likewise Beyoncé Knowles of Destiny's Child with her solo album.

XL admirably tried to remain defiant and positive. Their official press release said, "This record will be remembered - this is not hype. *Elephant* will make sense to people who gave up long ago. It's monumental. To celebrate the release... we've let our creative streak show. Literally. XL has redecorated the outside of the West London office in an instantly recognisable red and white candy cane swirl. Long may it last. Take a look." There seemed no end to the hype - there was even a (false) internet rumour that they were to be made into waxworks at Madame Tussauds!

As for official snippets of the album, the hype around the record ensured that these were also kept to a bare minimum. One consequence of this strict policing was a disagreement with John Peel. He related the unexpected tale to me: "Things took a strange twist when I got hold of a copy of *Elephant* and started playing it, because you get a record, it exists - you play it. Back in the awful period of the 1970s when all you had to look forward to was the possibility of there being a new Allman Bros LP before the year was out, part of the pleasure you got from doing a radio show was trying to get something fresh and new off the record companies. I was just playing The White Stripes' record because it was a good record and I wanted to play it. And then I was warned off. And as they haven't rescinded their warning I haven't played it.

It just seems disappointing really because I don't think that would have come from the band themselves. That's just what happens when you get involved with major labels, you know, they get into playing those sort of games with you. But fuck them, there's plenty of other stuff around as well. I can play old White Stripes records and I had all the pleasure of going through and trying to find all of the records that Jack White played on with his mates."

The band played a suitably low-key gig at the Electric Cinema in west London on February 7, 2003 for a brief but exhilarating five song set. Typically, Jack did not use the opportunity to play five brand new tracks, but instead sent the crowd back down the path to the blues, covering Led Zeppelin's 'In My Time Of Dying' and traditional folk favourite 'Blackjack Davey'. The two new tracks played were 'You've Got Her In Your Pocket' and the Meg vocal track, 'In The Cold, Cold, Night', the latter without the aid of a kit, a first for the shy White Stripes drummer. They closed with 'Hotel Yorba', which Jack quirkily introduced as "a song that was a hit on this island many years ago."

This very exclusive show had been a precursor to the aforementioned more public series of five dates starting in early April at the Wolverhampton Civic Hall and ending with two big shows at Brixton Academy all of which were sold out. They were supported by fellow Detroiters Whirlwind Heat and the Go. The former act was signed to Jack's own record label Third Man - he even produced Whirlwind Heat's debut long player. "It sounds amazing... they are extremely talented boys, and I think they are the new Devo."; the Go had an even closer ties to

Jack, as has been chronicled, but this certainly did not win them any favours with the press on these dates, least of all from *NME* who called their set "reprehensible Quo-isms".

Also enjoying a higher profile just prior to – and of course after – the release of the new Stripes album was Holly Golightly. Her appearance on 'It's True That We Love One Another', naturally turned the media's spotlight on to this relatively unknown cult singer. Like Dido before her with Eminem, Holly's musical career stretched back some years before her paths crossed with The White Stripes. Way back at the start of the 1990s, she was the singer-songwriter with the Headcoatees. She went solo in 1995, proceeding to release several solo records rooted very much in the blues and folk genres that so fascinated Jack too. Her first close contact with the Stripes came as support act to a show of theirs at the London Kentish Town Forum in December 2001. The Headcoatees were a splinter group from the similarly named the Headcoats, whose Bruce Brand would go on to help Jack design the artwork for the *Elephant* album. The Headcoats were at the forefront of a cluster of garage rock bands centred around the Dirty Water Club in London. One of the band, Billy Childish, was referenced by Jack White on *Top of the Pops* when his initial and surname were scrawled along the latter's right forearm in black marker pen.

And finally, so it came to pass that *Elephant* was released. Most observers had expected the album to solicit considerable acclaim, but no one could have guessed the extent of the applause, nor indeed the size of the subsequent commercial success.

The media hailed it as a classic, the album of the year and possibly of the decade so far. The commercial success mirrored this fervour. The album entered the UK charts at Number 1, thankfully knocking the sanitised nu-rock of Linkin Park off the top spot, selling over 65,000 in the process. Famed for their expensive videos and often criticised for their fabricated sound, Linkin Park would probably spend more mixing a single track then The White Stripes did on recording the entire *Elephant* album. In the same month, Robbie Williams' new album, *Escapology* - despite having sold over a million copies in the UK in double quick time - failed to chart in America, having sold just 21,000 in its first week. *Elephant* sold *six* times this amount, despite Robbie's album being heavily discounted (and the first record tied to a reputed £80 million record contract with EMI). The White Stripes must have struggled not to chuckle. No regrets indeed.

Cynics suggested that in an era when Eminem would shift *one million* albums in a week in the USA, these figures were hardly something to write home about, but nonetheless in the more muted commercial climate, post-Iraqi war, this was still an impressive achievement for the Detroit duo. Jack was as surprised as anyone when talking to *X-Ray* magazine two weeks after the album's release: "It's boggling my mind, I can't believe it's on the charts, let alone staying at the top." Also rather pleased was Liam Watson of Toe Rag, who would very soon be able to put his studio's very first platinum record up on his wall.

The mammoth commercial and critical success of *Elephant* means that The White Stripes are no longer just a garage rock band from Detroit. They are a globally huge act, whether they enjoy that status or not.

One proposed 'tour' date which unfortunately did not come off was a show inside a jumbo jet at 35,000 feet! The band's American label, V2, part of the Richard Branson empire, suggested the idea but sadly the logistics and exorbitant cost of the exercise rendered it impossible. Jack was initially ultra-excited by the concept but when it transpired it would take at least nine months to prepare the plane and the estimated costs of several million dollars for the one show would have to be subsidised by sponsorship from Virgin Mobile and Virgin Atlantic, he began to have reservations. In the end, the whole idea never literally got off the ground.

Back in the Fall of 2002, Jack White had won his first role in a feature film. Most stars would be happy with the acclaim and huge sales that their records had begun to enjoy, but for Jack White it seemed the next album was (once again) just one of many projects he had on the go at the same time. The film in question, *Cold Mountain* (based on Charles Frazier's book of the same name) was the story of a wounded Confederate soldier's odyssey from a hospital to his North Carolina home and the woman he left behind. Jack was also contributing songs to the soundtrack of the film.

Jack received a phone call from Anthony Minghella who wanted him to audition to play the role of Georgie, a Confederate soldier and musician on the run during this Civil War epic. Jack was initially put off by the supposedly high profile cast. Unlike many previous rockers who dabble in Hollywood circles, the cast of this movie suggested it was much more than just a celebrity whim: alongside Jack were also Brit actor Jude Law, Australian beauty Nicole Kidman and, most notably of all as far as The White Stripes fans were concerned, the waif-like real life alter-ego of Bridget Jones, Renee Zellweger - with whom Jack would soon start to have a relationship.

The plan was for his character to play 'Sittin' On Top Of The World' and 'Wayfaring Stranger' among other songs. For Jack, this was second nature: "'Sittin' On Top Of The World' was the first blues song I learned to play, from Howlin' Wolf's version, when I was a teenager actually, so I had known that. And I knew 'Wayfaring Stranger' from Two Star Tabernacle - we had played that song. So when I went to audition for the director, I already knew how to play that song."

Jack appears playing old American folk songs and this, as well as the fact he was recommended for the part by bluesman T-Bone Burnett, convinced him to take up the role. Jack told *Q* how he was happy he could use the film to bring American folk to a wider audience: "It's about the music. I was amazed to be chosen because... T-Bone Burnett could hear our roots go deeper, back to blues."

Although Jack was allocated his own driver for the duration of the shoot, the setting for the film was far from glamorous, right in the heart of Dracula terrain, Transylvania. As Jack told one magazine, it was a short, sharp shock to his system: "I was there for six weeks... freezing cold in the snow. I was on top of a hill a mile away and Renee Zellweger's down at the bottom herding sheep or something and she's laughing at me, 'Look at you rock star!' You're at the top of a hill and you've got to run down twenty times. As soon as I'd run down, I'd have to walk slowly right back up the hill and then as soon as I got there it was, 'OK, action!' That made me mad!"

Jack had the foresight to take his guitar with him in expectation of a lot of waiting around. Predictably he found himself alone in freezing cold hotel rooms for hours on end but, perhaps not surprisingly, the muse to write did not join him. Having hoped to come away with enough material for at least one album, he actually returned home with not one single song.

The duo did at least get to play some live material. Midway through the shoot, in November 2002, Meg joined Jack and the band played a rare low-key show in the Aro Palace Hotel in Brasov, Transylvania for the cast of the film plus about four hundred others. The film would later be released post-*Elephant*.

Jack did come back with one new development - that relationship with the superstar Zellweger. Rumours were initially seen as press hype but by the early summer of 2003 it became apparent that the two were indeed an item. Soon after, they would be seen out on the town together for the first time. Jack is notoriously shy around women and had this to say about the perils of finding Mrs Right/White given his unusual profile: "To keep a relationship going is constant work, you constantly have to fuel that fire to keep it alive. A lot of people disregard the rules and say, 'If you don't like what I do then forget it.' I think that's wrong. I think people should always be working on themselves."

This feature film was not The White Stripes only excursion into the celluloid world at this time. Later in 2003, both Jack and Meg were scheduled to appear in a short film directed by cult figure, Jim Jarmusch. He was pencilled in to direct a video for the band itself but before then had already cast them to act in one of his renowned movie miniatures, called *Coffee And Cigarettes*, reportedly alongside Iggy Pop and Steve Buscemi. The idea was just for Jack and Meg to talk to one another for five minutes - Jarmusch had done similarly peculiar mini-films with names such as Iggy Pop, Tom Waits and GZA and RZA of the Wu-Tang Clan.

Nor was this the band's first film work. They had previously appeared on the excellent *The Detroit Rock Movie* that features interviews with Jack in his room, shots of Jack White playing live with the Go, short footage of Meg playing the drums, an early version of 'The Union Forever' as well as interviews with Brendan Benson at his house and tons of other key players on the Detroit scene. It is an essential document for anyone interested in The White Stripes and the Detroit guitar scene.

On July 4, 2003, Jack was back at home in Detroit playing on stage with a hastily-formed band called the Science Farm at a gig at the city's Magic Stick venue. It was a party thrown to celebrate the opening of Dave Buick's new record store, called Young Soul Rebel Records. The Science Farm consisted of Jack, his cousin Ben Blackwell and long-time friend Brian Muldoon. Jack sang some songs but also played much of the set with his back to the crowd. One of the highlights of the gig was a cover of the Kingsmen's 1964 smash, 'Louie Louie'. Renee Zellweger was, not surprisingly, in the audience. What she and anyone else among the lucky few watching the small show was that would prove to be Jack's last gig of the summer, probably of the year and possibly... ever.

CHAPTER 16

"A lot of people never use their initiative because no one tells them to."

Mary Allen

At precisely 1pm on Jack's twenty-eighth birthday - July 9, 2003 - he received a most unwelcome present as he was driving through Detroit with his new girlfriend, Renée Zellweger. Jack's (red) vintage car was involved in an accident. Although the collision was at a modest speed and the scale of the accident itself was not too drastic, the impact was sufficient enough to break a finger on Jack's left hand – reports suggested it was actually his airbag and not the smash that did the damage (although vintage cars do not have airbags).

In a rather obtuse and rambling message on his own website (addressed to his "candy cane children"), Jack said a car pulled out in front of him and he was unable to brake in time to avoid an accident. After a hospital inspection, it transpired that Jack had suffered a compound triple fracture on the index finger. Not ideal when you play guitar for a living, but even more disastrous when you have a string of festival appearances and headlining shows lined up around the world to promote one of the year's most talked-about new albums. Coming after Meg's wrist injury in March, it was a cruel and bitter blow.

Jack was gutted about the cancelled dates but at the same time philosophical about the injury. He had talked in the media about how so many rock stars had died in their twenty-seventh year - Kurt Cobain, Jim Morrison, Jimi Hendrix, Janis Joplin - and he mused that by reaching 28 he had, in fact, "got off with just a warning."

Bizarrely, Jack decided to film the operation on his broken finger "for those admirers of the band with tickets to cancelled shows to better understand the complexity of the situation." Refreshing, to be fair, for an industry which often sees thousands of fans disappointed by cancelled shows only to be told their hero has that great intangible illness, 'nervous exhaustion', which often equates to the mother of all hang-overs or a drug binge.

Looking like something out of a TV show called *When Rock Stars Get Attacked!*, Jack was wheeled in and his finger duly pulled open and three metal pins inserted. These will remain with him for life and will no doubt cause much glee with airport customs officers every time the famous rock star walks through their metal detector gates. The procedure itself wasn't too surprising - what came as a shock was that Jack wasn't wearing regulation red or white.

On a serious note, the damaged finger needed months of intensive physiotherapy and even then may never be as mobile as prior to the accident. At one point, there was genuine concern for Jack being able to play guitar ever again. Even the most optimistic prognosis said a minimum of four weeks would be needed before Jack could even pick his guitar up (ironically, Jack has said that 'finger' and 'hand' are his two favourite lyrical words).

The history books show us that Jack was in good digit-mangling company. Jazz guitarist Django Reinhardt lost two fingers on his left hand in a fire and simply devised a new method of playing the guitar instead; Jerry Garcia and Black Sabbath's Tommy Lommi also had less than the full finger quota.

Despite this glorious company, Jack was obviously not able to honour the numerous high profile festival and other live shows that the band had scheduled to promote *Elephant* throughout the summer of 2003. These cancelled dates included, most immediately, a headline slot at the tenth anniversary T In The Park Festival and the Witness Festival too, plus an August north American tour, as well as festival shows such as the Reading and Leeds dates. Industry insiders speculated about the cost of losing such prestigious bookings and most felt that the T In The Park slot alone might have generated a fee of around £200,000.

Their top billing at T In The Park was handed down to the mercurial Flaming. Rather fabulously, Wayne Coyne and the rest of the Flaming Lips performed their last minute headline slot as a White Stripes tribute band. Known for their thrilling music but also for their irreverent live shows - including a *Top of the Pops* performance with pop kingpin Justin Timberlake dressed as a banana on bass) - the Lips took to the stage all dressed in red and white and covered in fake blood and flour!

Jack and Wayne had become good friends in the months leading up to this impromptu tribute set. They originally met backstage at a show in Detroit, where an admiring Jack handed Wayne (for some reason) a fibre optic statue of Jesus. Wayne reciprocated by writing a song about this called, naturally, 'Thank you Jack White (For The Fibre Optic Jesus That You Gave Me)'. Thus, when the Stripes literally crashed out of the T In The Park show, their Oklahoma friends were invited to step in.

To play at such late notice on such a high profile slot was one challenge - to completely re-organise their own set and revamp various Stripes tracks within a few short hours was staggering. "I don't know if every band looks for these kind of absurd moments, but they're what I live for," explained an excitable Wayne just prior to the show in *NME*. "We get to put on capes and do White Stripes songs... Luckily I had the red cape anyway. I keep stuff like that, you just never know when you might need it." In a set that was met with frenzied applause from an appreciative crowd of disappointed Stripes fans, the band also dedicated a madcap version of 'Happy Birthday' to Jack.

For The White Stripes themselves, the plan was to reschedule many of these shows for mid-to-late September, although clearly the festival opportunities had now passed. There was some talk of the band playing their own headline UK gigs with first availability going to Reading and Leeds Festival ticket holders by way of a worthy apology.

To keep their fans sated during this enforced live sabbatical, the band released the next single from *Elephant*, namely 'I Just Don't Know What To Do With Myself', on September 1, 2003. Although this song had sat well on the album, it was a very disappointing choice of single and easily their weakest for some time, arguably ever. The listener was hard put to avoid the feeling it was a deliberately contrary choice, but one that did little to enlighten fans and the wider public about The White Stripes. The track was backed with a cover of 'Who's To Say', written by Jack's friend Blanche as well as a Peel session version of 'I'm Finding It Harder To Be A Gentleman'. That said, it enjoyed a strong chart position and only served to strengthen sales of the album.

This single's success was hugely helped by the erotic accompanying video, directed by Sofia Coppola and starring a scantily-clad pole-dancing supermodel Kate Moss. The sizzling black and white footage guaranteed the band a sizeable splash of tabloid coverage. Long-term fan Moss, who'd attended that famous show at the Boston Arms, produced a raunchy performance which was described by *The Daily Mirror* as "one of the sexiest pop videos ever made". The paean to poles helped keep The White Stripes profile at an all-time high (although Jack seemed strangely reluctant to enthuse in the press saying "it was completely Sofia's idea"). Presumably this saucy idea was a concept and story board that came about after Jack's broken finger kept him out of action for so long - at least, we can only hope that Jack wasn't the original intended pole prancer. The mind boggles.

Typically, rather than sit at home doing nothing, Jack chose to convalesce in the only way he knew how - working on music. For much of his recovery time, he worked on production for country legend Loretta Lynn's new album in Nashville.

The band did not delay plans for their next single either, despite all this work. Even before 'I Just Don't Know What To Do With Myself' had been released, they were working on the video for their next release, 'The Hardest Button To Button' (other reports said it would be 'Black Math'), due out in America in the Fall of 2003. This time the video was directed by Michael Gondry - who also filmed 'Fell In Love...' and the 'Dirty Leaves..' videos - and featured more zoom photography similar to that found in 'Seven Nation Army'. Jack was not backwards in coming forwards about the results: "I think it is the greatest video we have ever made. I think it is one of the greatest videos ever made. I can't stop watching it, I've watched it fifty times."

As for the band's long term plans and potential, there is less certainty. Just as Coldplay were telling admirers that unless they could "reinvent the wheel" with their next album to follow up the stunning *Rush Of Blood To The Head*, they would call it a day, so it seemed that Jack and Meg were contemplating their future. What is more, they seemed even more pessimistic than Chris Martin, with some interviews quoting them as saying that *Elephant* may well be their last record ever. Invariably, however, the quotes were always taken just a little out of context, usually meant to say they would be reluctant to release anything that wasn't an improvement on their last.

He was, however, conjecturing about the longevity of his band just prior to the release of *Elephant*, telling *NME* that, "We both feel that a time is going to come when we don't think this will be relevant to ourselves. I think we should feel a clock ticking the whole time [Author's note - likely when your house if filled with a collection of clocks]. We're never going to try to beat a dead horse, do it for the money or to maintain some celebrity lifestyle. We've all seen bands we've loved over the years going through the motions... you just don't want to get to that point. You can't let popular perception invade your brain."

Having worked with The White Stripes from their very first album, producer Jim Diamond is perhaps best placed to conjecture about the direction of any future recordings, particularly with reference to the necessarily restrictive format of a guitar and drums only. "I don't know how you could record that way forever. That said, if they came to me and said, 'let's do exactly the same thing again', I'd get a kick out of it, it would be fun, but I don't know if they could keep doing that. I think they will have to change their approach. The difficulty is you have to be very careful about changing your approach, people get used to one style."

Detroit journalist Gary Graff is excited about the possibilities for future recordings: "The White Stripes could go any way they want, really, anywhere Jack wants. They could add musicians, although I don't think they ever will. If Jack ever worked in a larger band it would be a different band, because I think The White Stripes is always going to be a two person vehicle. He really is an original thinker, a real free thinker and he'll go places we never would have expected him to go. As for future material, the way he works I would never even hazard a prediction!"

DJ John Peel suggests the issues which might trouble The White Stripes are more to do with the machinations of the record business than with the evolution of their music. "There are very few people who have managed to survive this business. It is a killer, of course, sometimes literally so, and those big corportations can't afford to take risks. If a band is taking risks then that means the record compnay is taking risks as well. But record companies are only interested in certainties. But I don't think music can be treated that way."

Some outsiders speculated that Jack might turn his intensely private lyrics into more overt social and political statements, but he seemed to rule this out when speaking in the first week of March, 2003, to *The New York Times*: "When I was a teenager, I was really into voicing my political opinions. But I could never see anything coming from it. The people who were organizing the rallies and everything, I started to notice that they lived for dissatisfaction. And that is not me. The blues could be very political, you know - Leadbelly sang about Hitler. But I shy away from doing anything like that because I'm scared of novelty. I'm scared of having nowhere to go with it. A band like Rage Against The Machine, they were very angry and political, but it seems like they ran out of things to be angry about, so they had to go back and talk about Vietnam. It can be interesting, but is that what you want to do, get angry about things you didn't even experience?"

For his part, Jack confirms that The White Stripes is all about just him and his former wife. "If it was me and three other guys on stage I would have to attack music in a totally different way. If Meg's not there, her component that adds to it, if that's missing, I don't know what I'm going to do."

CHƎPTeꓳ 17

"Jim Morrison is dead now, and that is a high price to pay for immortality."

Back in Detroit, life goes on, still peculiar, still relevant. The Gold Dollar has closed down and Neil Yee has other projects to occupy his hyperactive mind. With the throbbing heart of the scene removed, the bands and players have gone elsewhere, found other hang-outs, other bars and clubs. With admirable objectivity, Neil Yee had no problem moving on from the golden days of his renowned venue: "When I started it, part of me was planning to do that for ever, but the problem was I had so many interests that gradually I started getting attracted to travelling and all kinds of other things. I just decided it wasn't my priority any more."

Interviewed for this book in July, 2003, Neil Yee was planning to start a record label, "called Cass Records which is after Cass Avenue where Gold Dollar was. Part of the plan is to do a compilation from Gold Dollar - a lot of these bands and their early recordings. I've made so many arbitrary decisions in my life and they've all seem to have worked out quite well. I had good fun doing it."

Yet the energy and drive of the city's guitar scene was far from over. The extent to which the Detroit scene had crystallised in both the eyes of the media and the actual bands involved had been displayed at a 'Christmas 2002 home-coming' show for many acts hosted by the Detroit CPOP Gallery, under the banner of 'Detroit City Sounds And Spirits'. Among the bill were the Waxwings, Ko Knockout, the Come Ons, Faith, Brendan Benson, the Soledad Brothers, Electric Six and, of course, Jack White.

It was actually a benefit gig spread across two stages situated in an art gallery - fitting considering the genesis of the scene at the eclectically - booked The Gold Dollar. Jack played a version of Elvis' 'One Night' while Meg just watched silently from the crowd, her place behind the kit taken by Soledad Brothers' Ben Swank (Meg has drummed for this band and was rumoured to be dating that outfit's Oliver).

Inevitably perhaps, the success of The White Stripes in particular, plus the heightened interest in Detroit bands generally, has meant that a certain corporate gloss has started to infect parts of the scene. Jack himself was a little concerned about this mainstream hijacking something so close to his heart. Speaking in 2003 he said, "Rock 'n' roll is back, in whatever form. The joke in our mind was always 'We'll take Detroit garage rock to the world.' We went to the mall a few months ago and they had 'garage rock'-cut jeans on sale."

He is not the only one to spot this worrying development. With the inevitable arrival of some cheque-book-waving A&R men who have only heard of The Gold Dollar and The White Stripes, there are understandable concerns that the essence of the Detroit scene will be lost. Mick Collins of the Gories and the Dirtbombs recalls how, "You would suddenly see these pony-tailed disasters walking around town handing out their business cards, that was scary, very silly. It had risen to a level of absurdity by then."

When *NME* ran a feature called 'A Very Rough Guide To Detroit' detailing the bests pubs, clubs and shops, many native Detroiters groaned. The magazine even invented a 'typical' Detroit musician called Johnny Kramer and listed what his typical day would be like. Other magazines' headlines such as "Is Detroit the new Seattle?" are merely laughable to those actually involved in the city's music scene.

Jeff Meier of Rocket 455 is less favourable to the scene post-White Stripes: "Music is my hobby, my sport, it's not my business. It just seemed like when The White Stripes hit, suddenly every band in town changed, the scene changed…drastically. The cool thing about living in Detroit had been the fact that no one gave a shit about anything, but since The White Stripes got big, it's like New York, you know. I guess there are plenty of people who think they're going to be the next Jack. But who would have thought that kid was going to be a superstar?

I always long for the old days kinda - but I guess I just fell through the cracks, when everything was hitting I decided that music was not going to be my main thing. I got a real job. I had to make some money, you know. My band did not see any beneficial impact after the success of The White Stripes. Some bands have, but not my band. Perhaps because I've made a point of separating myself from all the people making a fashion statement. This whole scene has built up and has got everybody thinking that they're going to make it too. I just kinda steer clear of all of that."

Mick Collins of the Gories and the Dirtbombs finds it perplexing that the term 'garage rock is used so much around these bands. "This current generation is not garage rock. They are not influenced by classic garage rock bands, their roots are not the same. The classic garage rock of the 1960s can almost entirely be traced back via the Stones, the Yardbirds and Pretty Things, then back through Chess Blues and so on. The latest bands are musically influenced almost completely by 1970s rock bands and even some 1990s Detroit bands which is worst of all."

Andy of Flying Bomb has little respect for the derivative acts he often sees. "Most of the bands that have come around since are mainly mimicking the likes of the Cobras, The White Stripes and so on. There's no versatility and I think they're all really boring. Detroit used to be really exciting, in fact most of the people I've known from the 1996/97 days, I don't see at shows too often. I rarely see people around anymore. I think it's kinda lost something."

He also rightly points out that the scene will likely survive in some form because so many of the key Detroit bands were already well-established: "Everyone pretty much was doing really good before 'the big jump' in England. For instance, we had bands like Bantam Rooster, the Dirtys, the Cobras, the Volcanoes had been around forever… so everybody already had records out." Yet he admits that there have been outsiders muscling in: "I've been places where I've heard people say they're from Detroit and find out they're from the other side of the state!"

Surge Joebot adds the view that continual reincarnations of bands and new acts keeps the scene vibrant: "You know nothing can last forever. But it's weird because we're in perhaps the fourth phase of this scene since 1995/6. It's continually dying and then picking up again in a slightly different form. Admittedly, The Gold Dollar closing was a huge drag that probably did more to kill the scene back then as I remember it."

Looking back, Andy of Flying Bomb cites the city's festival in the summer of 1997 as his peak of this incarnation of Detroit music: "That festival was overwhelming. We had everybody playing and with hindsight we just didn't realise that was probably the highest point. Right after that everybody seemed to start breaking up and it fell apart which was kinda sad. The Duties broke up, the Cobras broke up, Rocket 455 broke up. Just out of nowhere it had gotten so big round here and then suddenly it broke up and just completely died. Even when people gradually started getting back together it seemed to be some of the same bands with different members."

Jim Diamond remains positive and insists this is still a relatively untapped source of rich talent in the city: "The mainstream's only really gotten hold of The White Stripes, so there's still plenty of other bands. I don't think the scene's peaked, no. There's only really been one band that's come out of here and gotten any real big exposure and they were together for four years before they got noticed on that level."

Jim also points out the success of the Von Bondies (whose Marcie spent a while dating Jack) and Electric Six. There are, of course, scores of other fascinating bands in the city. The 313 phone code area seems to have more achingly primitive rock bands than much of the world put together. To feature them all would command another book entirely, but namechecks must go out to the Von Bondies and the Go, who both finally began to make some waves abroad in 2002-3; the Clone Defects add an edge of metal to proceedings; Slumber Party have been described as "borderline shoegazers"; the Come Ons play more traditional 1960s guitar rock-pop; the Dirtbombs bridge the gap between glam, Motown and the blues and, rather brilliantly, just about any other genre you might care to mention; the Piranhas are essentially a punk band, assured the status of local legends for their infamous 'rat show' at The Gold Dollar in 1999 when their singer performed with a bloody, freshly executed rat duct-taped to his naked torso; The Detroit Cobras are Detroit guitar music at its finest; the Hentchmen remain one of the most important guitar bands of the 1990s; Whirlwind Heat began to enjoy much publicity in 2003, helped by Jack White's aforementioned production duties; and the Paybacks, led by writer and rock goddess Wendy Case will, if justice prevails, also come to enjoy their share of the musical limelight. And there are dozens more...

As for how The White Stripes are perceived back in Detroit, the general feeling is congratulatory. Ben Blackwell feels that people are more than happy to see The White Stripes break out of Detroit and do so well: "People are really proud of them. As far as the people who have known about them for a long time, such as Dave Buick and the Hentchmen, those people just treated them like it's old times, you know."

Gary Graff explains his view of Jack and Meg's reputation since their chart success: "There's a lot of regard for Jack and that mitigates any of the terminally hip attitude you might otherwise see around an underground band who have enjoyed mainstream success. He has helped a lot of bands locally too, they've put a lot of bands on their shows and he's done some production for them too. They've been good members of the community and not gloated on their success. They're still largely the same people they were prior to their success. He still likes to go youth record shopping and they still hang out in a lot of the same places." [Authors Note: Jack has worked with countless Detroit bands and acts from other locations: he appears on the self-released 'Master Supertone' CS by Soledad Brothers; on the 'Some Other Guy' seven inch and the *Hentch-Forth* twelve inch release and the 'Ham And Oil' single by the Hentchmen; on 'Johnny's Death Letter' by the Soledad Brothers' 'Sugar & Spice' single; produced the debut and second single and debut album by the Von Bondies; mixed 'The Gospel According To John' single by Soledad Brothers; co-mixed a Greenhornes single; appears on 'Shout Bama Lama' by the Detroit Cobras; appears on a track called 'Mystery Man' by the Thee Jenerators, recorded at Toe Rag; and he can be heard playing on the debut album of DJ Mark Ronson, son of legendary guitarist and Bowie cohort Mick.]

Andy of Flying Bomb has a different perspective on the subject of Jack and Meg distancing themselves from their Detroit beginnings. When Andy was in the process of compiling a new Christmas sampler in 2002, he states he was told by their record label that Jack did not want to be included on compilations anymore. "I think Jack's kinda paranoid about stuff, he just says everybody's trying to take advantage of him. And that's just kinda bothersome to me because people like Flying Bomb were involved early on. A lot of people I still talk to who have done very well outside of Michigan are still the same people I've always known. I never see Meg anymore but Jack, you know, it's just like he treats us like we're fans or something. It is definitely annoying because we were always so supportive, even up 'till lately you know, it was great. We were always super proud and said, 'You're doing good, you deserve it.' Then something like that happens and it's like, 'Uh?' It just deflates you."

Yet Jack seemed acutely aware that his home-grown friends would never tolerate any rock star aloofness: "We have friends, people in Detroit who, if you were to wake up every morning and say, 'Hey guess what? We're Number 1!'… they'd be really turned off by it. Even if we wanted to share that, it would be really difficult, but that's a good thing because that keeps us humble about everything." Some of them have even begun to do Jack White impressions!

Jeff Meier related to me how Jack's parents held a fiftieth wedding anniversary party in the summer of 2003, and he explained what a nice party Jack held for them at the church hall where he belonged when he was a kid. Renee Zellweger was there, but this was no snotty rock-star-brings-actress-wife incident. "I ran into him the other day and he said the party was real fun with the neighbours hanging out and nobody was acting star struck. Everybody was just normal."

It is convenient to categorize The White Stripes as a successful modern hybrid of punk and the blues, which are after all two of the most raw and explosive forms of music. Some even say they have taken blues "to the masses" (worst of all is the phrase 'modern white blues'). But there is so much more to the band than such a straight-forward summary as that, as events within this tale have shown. Have they morphed the blues into something modern and altogether more intriguing? Perhaps, perhaps not. What they have done is take their music – a blender of some of the most unusual and demanding genres of all-time – to a mass audience that even the most optimistic Stripes fan could never have forseen.

The White Stripes are probably a band that could only have come from Detroit. Its multitude of musical styles, melting pot of cultures, labile social and political history and segregated yet sociable community spirit have all played crucial roles in the creation of the band. Whether you agree that a band is a product of its environment or is solely creditable for its success and muse is a philosophical argument for another time. Suffice to say, without Detroit, there would probably have been no White Stripes. And for that, we must be eternally grateful.

DISCOGRAPHY

ALBUMS

The White Stripes

Jimmy The Exploder / Stop Breaking Down / The Big Three Killed My Baby (CD only) / Suzy Lee / Sugar Never Tasted So Good (CD only) / Wasting My Time / Cannon / Astro / Broken Bricks / When I Hear My Name / Do / Screwdriver / One More Cup Of Coffee (CD only) / Little People / Slicker Drips / St. James Infirmary Blues / I Fought Piranhas
Japanese Edition included Let`s Shake Hands & Lafayette Blues as bonus tracks
CD, LP – Sympathy for the Record Industry 1999

De Stijil

You're Pretty Good Looking (For A Girl) / Hello Operator / Little Bird / Apple Blossom / I'm Bound To Pack It Up / Death Letter / Sister, Do You Know My Name? / Truth Doesn't Make A Noise / A Boy's Best Friend / Let's Build A Home / Jumble, Jumble / Why Can't You Be Nicer To Me? / Your Southern Can Is Mine
CD, LP – Sympathy for the Record Industry 2000

White Blood Cells

Dead Leaves And The Dirty Ground / Hotel Yorba / I'm Finding It Harder To Be A Gentleman / Fell In Love With A Girl / Expecting / Little Room / The Union Forever / The Same Boy You've Always Known / We're Going To Be Friends / Offend In Every Way / I Think I Smell A Rat / Aluminum / I Can't Wait / Now Mary / I Can Learn / This Protector
CD, LP – XL / V2 2001

White Blood Cells

Dead Leaves And The Dirty Ground / Hotel Yorba / I'm Finding It Harder To Be A Gentleman / Fell In Love With A Girl / Expecting / Little Room / The Union Forever / The Same Boy You've Always Known / We're Going To Be Friends / Offend In Every Way / I Think I Smell A Rat / Aluminum / I Can't Wait / Now Mary / I Can Learn / This Protector
Bonus DVD: Video - Dead Leaves And The Dirty Ground / Fell In Love With A Girl / Hotel Yorba / We're Going To Be Friends / Audio - Lafayette Blues / Hand Springs
CD/DVD - V2 2002

Elephant

Seven Nation Army / Black Math / There's No Home For You Here / I Just Don't
Know What To Do With Myself / It's Cold, Cold, Night / I Want To Be With The Boy
You've Got Her In Your Pocket / Ball And Biscuit / The Hardest Button To Button
/ Little Acorns / Hypnotize / The Air Near My Fingers / Girl You Have No Faith In
Medicine / It's True That We Love One Another
Japanese Edition contained the bonus tracks Who's To Say & Good To Me
CD, LP – XL/V2 2003

SINGLES

Let's Shake Hands/ Look Me Over Closely
7" – Italy 1997

Lafayette Blues / Sugar Never Tasted So Good
7" – Italy 1998

Hand Springs
7" – Multiball Records 2000

The Big Three Killed My Baby / Red Bowling Ball Ruth
7" – Sympathy For The Record Industry 2000

Hello Operator / Jolene
7" – Sympathy For The Record Industry 2000

Lord Send Me An Angel / You're Pretty Good Looking (Trendy American Remix)
7" – Sympathy For The Record Industry 2000

Party Of Special Things To Do / China Pig / Ashtray Heart
7" – Subpop 2000

Hotel Yorba / Rated X
CD – XL 2001

Hotel Yorba / Hotel Yorba (Live At Hotel Yorba) / Rated X (Live At Hotel Yorba) /
Hotel Yorba (Enhanced Video)
CD – XL 2001

Hotel Yorba (Live At The Hotel Yorba) / Rated X (Live At The Hotel Yorba)
7" – XL 2001

Red Death At 6:14 [Promo]
7" – XL 2002

We're Going To Be Friends
CD – V2 2002

Fell In Love With A Girl / Let's Shake Hands / Lafayette Blues
CD – XL 2002

Fell In Love With A Girl / Lovesick (Live At The Forum) / I Just Don't Know What
To Do With Myself / Fell In Love With A Girl (Enhanced Video)
CD – XL 2002

Fell In Love With A Girl / I Just Don't Know What To Do With Myself
7" – XL 2002

Candy Cane Children / The Reading Of The Story Of The Magic / The Singing Of
Silent Night
7" – Third Man/V2 2002

Dead Leaves And The Dirty Ground / Suzy Lee / Stop Breaking Down
CD – XL 2002

Dead Leaves And The Dirty Ground / Stop Breaking Down
7" – XL 2002

Dead Leaves And The Dirty Ground / Fell In Love With A Girl / Hotel Yorba
[Promo]
CD – Sympathy For The Record Industry 2002

White Blood Cells Bonus Tracks: Jolene / Hand Springs / Hotel Yorba (Live)
Love Sick (Live) [Promo]
CD - V2 2002

Seven Nation Army / Good To Me / Black Jack Davey
CD – XL 2003

Elephant Sampler - Seven Nation Army / In The Cold, Cold Night
7" – XL 2003

7 Nation Army / Good To Me
7" – XL 2003

I Just Don't Know What To Do With Myself / Lafayette Blues / Black Math
CD 1 - XL 2003

I Just Don't Know What To Do With Myself / Who's To Say / I'm Finding It Harder
To Be A Gentleman [Live on John Peel show]
CD 2 – XL 2003

I just Don't Know What To Do With Myself / Who's To Say
7" – XL 2003

SPLIT SINGLES

It takes Two, Baby: Mr. Airplane Man - Hangin' Round Your Door / The White
Stripes - Fell In Love With A Gir1 / Rizzo – Cathy / Bantam Rooster - Shitlist + 1
7" – Sympathy For The Record Industry 2001

Surprise Package – Rocket 455 – Santa Ain't Coming For Christmas / The
Blowtops – Sidewalk Santa / The White Stripes – Candy Cane Children
7" – Flying Bomb Records 1998

BOOTLEGS

WDET Radio Session - 3/2/1999

Banter / Sugar Never Tasted So Good / Banter / The Big Three Killed My Baby /
Do / Banter / Jimmy The Exploder / Banter / Screwdriver / Banter / Dead Leaves
And The Dirty Ground / Banter
CD

Vincent's Ear, Asheville NC - 29/9/2000

Let's Shake Hands / When I Hear My Name / Big Three Killed My Baby / Cannon
/ Jolene / Death Letter / Little Bird / Your Pretty Good Looking (For A Girl) / Hello
Operator / Do / Your Southern Can Is Mine / Sugar Never Tasted So Good / Astro
/ Jack The Ripper / Broken Bricks / Dead Leaves And The Dirty Ground / Jimmy
The Exploder / Truth Doesn't Make A Noise / Wasting My Time / One More Cup
Of Coffee / Apple Blossom / Look Me Over Closely / Jumble, Jumble / Lord, Send
Me An Angel / Screwdriver
CD

Jack White Solo

Garden Bowl Bar, Detroit, MI - 3/6/2001
Hotel Yorba / Rated X / Cold Brains / I'm Finding It Harder To Be A Gentleman /
Fragile Girl / Dyin' Crapshooter's Blues / Black Jack Davey / In My Time Of Dyin'
(Jesus Make Up My Dying Bed) / Lord, Send Me An Angel / Home, Sweet Home /
Who's To Say / We're Gonna Be Friends / The Same Boy You've Always Known /
Baby Blue
CD

Chicago IL - 7/6/2001

Let's Shake Hands / When I Hear My Name / Jolene (Dolly Parton cover) / Dead
Leaves And The Dirty Ground / Hotel Yorba / I Think I Smell A Rat / Union Forever
/ Offend In Every Way / We Are Going To Be Friends / Pretty Good Looking /
Hello Operator / Death Letter / Let's Build A Home / I Fought Piranahs / Lafayette
Blues / Broken Bricks / Cannon / Screwdriver / Wasting My Time / Your Southern
Can Is Mine / Stop Breaking Down
CD

The Point, Oxford, London - 29/7/2001

Let's Shake Hands / When I Hear My Name / Wasting My Time / Your Pretty
Good Looking (For A Girl) / Dead Leaves & The Dirty Ground / Jolene / Hotel
Yorba / Lord, Send Me An Angel / Death Letter / The Union Forever / We're
Going To Be Friends / Apple Blossom / I Think I Smell A Rat / Screwdriver / Hello
Operator / Look Me Over Closely
CD

Pop Attack Festival, Barcelona, Spain - 1/11/2001

Let's Shake Hands / Dead Leaves & The Dirty Ground / Jolene / I'm Finding It
Harder To Be A Gentleman / Stop Breaking Down / Fell In Love With A Girl / Little
Room / The Union Forever / Your Southern Can Is Mine / Apple Blossom / Your
Pretty Good Looking (For A Girl) / Hotel Yorba / Look Me Over Closely
CD

Forum, London, England - 06/12/2001

Fell In Love With A Girl / When I Hear My Name / I Think I Smell A Rat / Dead
Leaves And Dirty Ground / Sick Of Love / Expecting / Little Room / Union Forever
/ Jolene / I'm Finding It Harder To Be A Gentleman / Hotel Yorba / Isis / You're
Pretty Good Looking / We Are Going To Be Friends / Apple Blossom / Astro / Jack
The Ripper / Rated X / Screwdriver
CD

The White Stripes - Peel Session, Radio 1 - 2001

Let's Shake Hands / When I Hear My Name / Jolene / Death Letter / Cannon
/ Astro / Hotel Yorba / I'm Finding It Hard / Screw Driver / We're Going To Be
Friends / You're Pretty Good Lucking / Hello Operator / Baby Blue
CD

Live at BBC Maida Vale - 2001

Look Me Over Closely / Lord, Send Me An Angel / Lovesick (Live at the Forum) /
Party of Special Things to Do / Why Don't We All Just Samba
CD

Union Square, New York, NY – 1/10/2002

Big Three Killed My Baby / Dead Leaves / Jolene / Apple Blossom / Pretty Good
Looking / Hello Operator / Lord Send Me An Angel / Hotel Yorba / Love Sick /
We're Going To Be Friends / Rated X / Sugar Never Tasted So Good / Death
Letter / Stones In My Passway / Astro / Farmer John / Louie Louie / Screwdriver
/ St James / Screwdriver / Teenage Head / Screwdriver / Grinnin In Your Face /
Screwdriver / For The Love Of Ivy / Boll Weevil
CD

Reading Festival, United Kingdom - 29/8/2002

Dead Leaves And The Dirty Ground / When I Hear My Name / I Think I Smell
A Rat / Jolene / Hotel Yorba / Apple Blossom / Jimmy The Exploder / Wayfaring
Stranger (Patty Griffen Cover) / Cannon / For The Love Of Ivy (The Gun Club
Cover) / Screwdriver / Empty Bottle
CD

The White Stripes, Lupo's, Providence, RI - 3/4/2002

Intro / Dead Leaves And The Dirty Ground / I Think I Smell A Rat / Apple
Blossom / When I Hear My Name / Hotel Yorba / Finding It Harder To Be A
Gentleman / Your Pretty Good Looking (For A Girl) / Hello Operator / Death Letter
/ Love Sick / We're Going To Be Friends / Fell In Love With A Girl / Offend In
Every Way / Lord, Send Me An Angel / Rated X / Astro / Jack The Ripper / Let's
Shake Hands / Look Me Over Closely / Screwdriver / Let's Build A Home / Little
Room / The Union Forever / Boll Weevill
CD

Orpheum Theatre, Boston, MA, USA - 20/04/03

Black Math / Dead Leaves And The Dirty Ground / Let's Shake Hands / I Think I
Smell A Rat / Party Of Special Things To Do (Captain Beefheart Cover) / Jolene
(Dolly Parton Cover) / Hardest Button To Button / Look Me Over Closely (Marlene
Dietrich Cover) / Apple Blossom / You're Pretty Good Looking / In The Cold, Cold,
Night / Death Letter (Son House Cover) / Motherless Children Have A Hard Time
(Blind Willie Johnson) / Red Bird (Leadbelly Cover) / Fell In Love With A Girl /
Don't Blame Me (Everly Brothers) / Hotel Yorba / Lord, Send Me An Angel (Blind
Willie Mctell) / Ball And Biscuit / Astro / Jack The Ripper (One Way Streets) /
Seven Nation Army / Boll Weevil (Leadbelly)
CD

White Stripes - Rarities Vol. 1

Apple of My Eye / Candy Cane Children / Hussy / I Ain't Superstitious / Jack
the Ripper / I Just Don't Know What To Do With Myself (w/Steve Lamacq) / Red
Bowling Ball / Ruth / Ashtray Heart / Buster (featuring the Strokes) / China Pig /
Handsprings / Jolene / Lafayette Blues / Let's Shake Hands
CD

Nobody Knows How To Talk To Children

Singles, B-Sides And Other Rare Tracks
Red Death At 6:14 / Jolene / Let's Shake Hands / Look Me Over Closely / Red
Bowling Ball Ruth / Lafayette Blues / Lord Send Me An Angel Down / China Pig
/ Ashtray Heart / Party Of Special Things To Do / Hand Springs / Candy Cane
Children / Apple Of My Eye / I Ain't Superstitious / Pain (Give Me Sympathy) /
Your Pretty Good Looking (Live) / Let's Shake Hands (Live) / When I Hear My
Name (Live) / Jolene (Live) / Your Southern Can Is Mine (Live) / Screwdriver (Live
- Late Show)
CD

B-Sides & Rarities

I Just Don't Know What To Do / Hotel Yorba (Live at Room 286 in the Hotel Yorba, Detroit) / Shaky Puddin' (The Soledad Brothers, Backing Vocals by Jack White) / Cadillac Hips (The Soledad Brothers, Recorded by Jack White, with Meg White on Percussion) / Sugar And Spice (The Soledad Brothers, recorded by Jack White, with Meg White on Percussion) / Gimme Back My Wig (The Soledad Brothers, recorded by Jack White, with Meg White on Percussion) / Sound Of Terror (The Von Bondies, recorded by Jack White) / Red Death at 6:14 / Hand Springs / Red Bowling Ball Ruth / Rated X (Live at Room 286 in the Hotel Yorba, Detroit) / Lafayette Blues / Candy Cane Children / Let's Shake Hands / The Henchmen (with Jack White) / Some Other Guy / Psycho Daisies
CD

INDEX

Photos courtesy of

Redferns
Live
Doug Coombe

NOTE ABOUT THE AUTHOR

Martin Roach gained a degree in Historical Research before starting his own publishing company, I.M.P. in 1992. Since then he has penned over 80 works on music, youth culture, celebrity and film. Editions of his work have been sold to the USA, France, Germany, Italy, Czechoslovakia, Slovenia, Croatia, Australia, New Zealand, Belgium, Norway, Holland, South Africa, Japan, Canada, Hong Kong, UAE and Brazil.

He lectures on, and has written numerous articles, essays and critiques about, music, songwriting, pop and youth culture (including So You Want To Be A Pop Star and NME Top 100 Singles). He has been invited to talk on scores of radio and television shows including BBC 2, ITV, BBC Radio 1, 2, 4 and 5, Xfm, countless regional BBC and commercial stations and many print media interviews. In 1999 he undertook a three week promotional tour of the USA and Europe to support his Dr Martens book.

Martin has to date written biographies of: Coldplay, The Strokes, Eminem, Korn, Limp Bizkit, Marilyn Manson, Manic Street Preachers, Destiny's Child, Radiohead, Madonna, REM, Jennifer Lopez, Kid Rock, Nirvana, Pearl Jam, Primal Scream and Nine Inch Nails.